The Male Awakening:

A Global Perspective

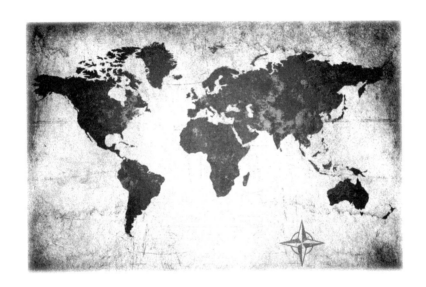

Rob Fournier

The Male Awakening: A Global Perspective

© 2019 by Rob Fourier
All rights reserved.

To learn more about Rob Fournier's work, please contact him through his website: TheRobFournier.com

Library of Congress Cataloging-in-Publication Data

Fournier, Rob
The Male Awakening: A Global Perspective

ISBN: 978-1-5136-4617-6 Paperback

ISBN: 978-1-5136-4618-3 eBook

1. OCC019000 - Body, Mind, Spirit: Inspiration & Personal Growth
2. TRV010000 - Travel: Essays & Travelogues
3. SEL021000 - Self-Help: Motivational & Inspiration

Empowered Whole Being Press
www.EmpoweredWholeBeingPress.com

Acknowledgments

I would like to thank each individual man who was open and willing to share his personal story within the pages of this book. By sharing your individual story, it will hopefully inspire others to follow their own truths. Your dedication allowed the vision of this book to come to fruition.

I would also like to thank all the dear souls that I call family. "Family" is a term that has shifted for me over the years. It started out with blood relatives but has now shifted to include everyone that I encounter. Each interaction creates a larger family and unity of community. Some of you followed my journey around the globe, and I greatly appreciate each one of you. Your underlying love carried me through on the tough days and kept me soaring on others. We are all in this journey together.

Lastly, I would like to thank Bailey Puppel for her efforts of making the final edits for this book.

Table of Contents

Introduction

Awakening. What does that mean? According to Google dictionary:

Noun

   1. An act of waking from sleep.

   2. An act or movement of becoming suddenly aware of something.

Adjective

   1. Coming into existence or awareness.

We all have our own interpretation of what "awakening" means to each of us. From my perspective, it is just that: a "waking up" and becoming aware of a new existence. When we learn something new, we wake up to a new truth – a new truth that may challenge old beliefs, but one that can also allow us to become more authentic. Being more authentic means allowing ourselves to follow our own path that is right for us, not one that we thought we should follow or one that was imposed on us.

When we have this new truth spark within the depths of ourselves, something occurs. It is a moment in which it feels like a light bulb has been turned on. A deep understanding occurs with a feeling of excitement, wonder, and peace – a place of knowing like we have never experienced before. Not a knowing that has been taught to us, but a deeper knowing of connection and trust.

As these new truths shine upon us, it shifts our current realities as we know it. This allows for new opportunities and growth to occur within and around us. Awakenings = new truths = new possibilities.

1

Awakenings, moments when we become aware of new truths, occur on a daily basis if we are open to witnessing them. However, most of us often only see the larger ones that occur. The larger events that happen in our life, such as a death of a loved one or personal illness, really get our attention. When they get our attention, things can begin to shift in a new direction – a direction that is more in alignment with our highest and greatest good.

As a male (the youngest of four children and the only boy) growing up in a middle-class American family, I learned certain roles about what it meant to be a boy and what the masculine identity entailed. My father was not one to express his emotions or cry in front of anyone, even at a funeral. This is what I learned that a male was supposed to do. Here are some of the beliefs I held, at the time, of what a male was supposed to do: be strong (which meant to not show emotions, to not talk about them, and to not be vulnerable), support your family, work hard, be a provider, work hard (yes, I listed it twice on purpose), create a family, and not to be supportive of open and healthy communication regarding feelings. I love my dad, however, his famous line in our house was, "Why are you crying? I will give you something to cry about!" This statement alone does not allow for open and supportive communication. Another line often used was, "You live in my house and these are my rules." Where do these "rules" come from. They come from what we learn to be true and adopt as our story through society and our family upbringing. My dad grew up in a very strict religious family house; hence where all the "rules" came from. He was acting in a way that he only knew to be true at the time. This is what I was learning from my family dynamics, as well as from society as a whole. I was learning that it was a sign of weakness to be vulnerable, to show your emotions or express your feelings in an open and supportive way. Instead, I was supposed to put on a show, pretending that all was well and I was happy. This is what society was teaching me.

Thankfully, I did not fit that paradigm. I was a very sensitive child. I did express my emotions, and I cried when upset. I often had contradictions between what I was "supposed to do" as a "male" and what I felt. I eventually learned to cry in my room by myself, falling into the paradigm that it was not okay to show my emotions, as it would be a sign of weakness. As my life would evolve, however, I would eventually have experiences that would allow me to reawaken to my truth and innocence that I remembered having before the social programming began. This is discussed further in Chapter 1.

As I began to have awakening moments of truth, I began to be free to be me, without fear or judgment of what I "should" be. Things quickly began to shift and change. One thing that shifted and changed was the purpose of my traveling. I first began to travel with friends, beginning in high school. We were much younger then, and our focus was on having a good time and partying. We shared many good memories. However, as this shift occurred within me, I began to travel for a different purpose. I noticed that my travels began centering instead on sacred sites around the world. I was encountering a new perspective and meeting new individuals that were in direct alignment with this internal shift I was experiencing.

Each subsequent destination easily aligned. I knew I was going to sacred sites at the time, but I did not see the grander picture of it all until recently. While traveling, I only trusted my inner guidance and knew that I would be shown the big picture when I needed to know. Well, that time is now. Each time I was guided to a different area of the world, I came across an individual guy who shared his own unique awakening experience. I was being guided to these places to connect with each man so that I can now share his unique, valuable perspective in this book.

Each guy I met touched my heart so deeply with his story and the way that he, too, was living his truth and passion. I saw an awakening occur within the male perspective that I once saw so differently. Here I was, halfway around the world, and men were experiencing the same thing I was in their own unique ways. Independently but also collectively, we were breaking free from the male consciousness that it is a sign of weakness for a man to share his feelings or to have an experience that is outside what others would consider the "norm." As I expressed my own personal story so openly and freely, I saw a shift in those around me. I was attracting others that were open and ready to share their stories, too.

I am forever grateful for trusting and being guided to all the amazing places around the world that I have been led too. At each place, I met these phenomenal men who are living examples of a shift in consciousness and awareness. Men who are assisting in shifting the perspective of what it means to be a male. Men who are showing that, when they share their emotions and experiences, they are revealing an even deeper strength beneath that. This revelation breaks down the barriers that we all might have once had (or may continue to have). It allows for a new truth to begin – a truth that we are all one.

The beauty of this book is that it shares the perspective of men from all around the globe, each one coming from a different region, family background, religion, and upbringing. All these things I just listed are labels. However, they show that even despite what we consider labels, underneath we are all having similar experiences. Labels and stories from our pasts do not define who we are. Through the course of this book, we break the illusion of labels. The labels that we create can separate us, even the label and illusion of what it is to be a male. Behind it all, we are all one. We are one creation and one living consciousness.

As you read through the book, you can see I came to encounter many beautiful souls, both men and women. However, throughout my journey, I received clear guidance on the message behind this book: a message to assist with the shift of male perspective. To allow the reader, like you, to read these individual stories and to see if one resonates with you. To assist other men in following their own truths – truths that are right for them. I encourage you to be open to allowing the vulnerability of these men sharing their stories to spark an awakening within yourself.

Being on the path of self-discovery for many years has led me to many lectures, leaders, and events. When attending these events, I have observed many things. The guys that were open to sharing their stories were generally the ones who were the presenters, taking leadership roles. There were many women presenters as well. However, among the attendees, approximately 80% were female and 20% male. Where were the other guys in the audience? For a long time, self-discovery has been more open within a female perspective; however, again, things are beginning to shift. This book shows the start of that: the self-discovery and awakening moments of different men from around the globe.

I have set up this book to show how I was guided to each area around the globe over the years, how I trusted in my inner guidance around the twists and turns, and how it led me to the exact right place, at the exact right time, to meet the exact right person. It then flows into the personal story of each individual guy sharing his own unique perspective of his own awakening moment, and what it means to him. All the men wrote their own stories, sharing their own unique characters, as you will see when their voices emerge.

As you read through each individual story, you will begin to understand for yourself how awakening occurs on many levels. Some of the men in the book are just beginning to awaken to their truth as they shed their old paradigms. Other men in the book have been on this road to awakening for quite some time as they share their deeper insights and wisdoms. Each one of us are on different paths and levels of understanding, all perfect in our own way. The infinite beauty is to show these varying levels within this book. The broader perspective allows for a deeper understating of the entirety of the male awakening.

Since each guy wrote his own story, I left each story in its original format with minimal editing. I wanted to allow for the authenticity of each speaker. This allows you to hear each unique voice. Each individual has a style of his own, which blends into the beauty of this book. I honor each person and his own unique style. I felt that if I edited their contributions, it would take away from the personal touch each one so delicately shared. Therefore, it was left to its original text for a purpose. As you will notice in their writings, English is not the first language for some of these men. Again, I left their text and messages as they were written to allow for authenticity.

Sharing your personal story can bring up many emotions and feelings – some of which I just discussed, such as expectations of being a male and the old paradigm. Even as I wrote this book, I worked through my own personal challenges so that I could share the bigger messages of this project. Many of the guys writing chapters in this book shared with me the struggles that they, too, experienced. These are all individuals who shared in an awakening moment, and yet are still struggling with sharing their truths. This is real. This is truth. However, each one took accountability for what was occurring, and that is the difference – the difference of noticing what is occurring within you, working with it, and allowing yourself to honor where you are. I am sharing this aspect of the book to show the reality of its creation. Just because you have an awakening moment does not mean that you do not still work through your own personal incongruences on a regular basis. However, it may get easier with time as you begin to take responsibility and accept the understanding that you are a co-creator of your life. That is where the true beauty lies.

Even with support, four guys in this book were not ready to share their story when the time came to write. I still included one of the chapters within the text of the book in order to show the reality of the current struggles we may face. He had a beautiful light when I met him and was excited to be part of the project, but found himself unable to write his personal awakening moment when the time came, even with dictation and coaching provided. I find this beautiful in its own creation, as he is still very much part of this book project. He allowed for a new aspect to shine and be shared with you.

Some of the men intertwine throughout the book, as our paths continued to cross on my journeys.

If you have gotten this far, I want to say thank you for purchasing this book, for being open to a new perspective, and for being part of the shift. We are all on this journey together.

Much love and many blessings,

Rob

1

Metro Detroit, Michigan
Rob's Awakening Moment

Hello, my name is Rob Fournier. I am from the metro Detroit area of Michigan in the United States; however, I recently moved to Laguna Beach, California. I grew up with three older sisters – I was the youngest and the only boy. I feel very blessed, as we are all still very close to this day. When we were growing up, there was always some kind of family event or function happening. We would all get together for holidays, each person's birthday (including cousins), and to just hang out. As the youngest, I learned to go with the flow around me the best I could.

I earned a degree in occupational therapy, and I have worked with pediatrics for over twenty years. I worked in various settings, including children's hospitals, private sensory integration clinics for children with autism and other developmental challenges, home care, and, lastly, a school district. I was introduced to CranioSacral Therapy during my career, through which I expanded my skills. I found a new passion within this work – so much so that, over time, I opened a wellness center with two friends that focused on offering this transformational work. In addition to private sessions, I also offered and led laughter yoga groups and shamanic sound immersion meditations. I found tremendous growth and potential with laughter, sound, vibration, and their effects on the body.

During this time, I was guided to publish my first book, *The Process: Soul's Journey to Oneness*. The book describes in more detail my own personal awakening, as well as the tools and tips I used (and continue to use) to guide myself on this discovery – one of those tools being CranioSacral Therapy. In the book, I share my personal stories of what transpired, as well as inspirations I received during my sessions and how I used those to self-heal.

"So," you may ask, "what sparked your awakening of greater consciousness?" My awakening has gradually unfolded on multiple levels. It all started at birth. I laugh even as I type this, as it sounds like a journey through time. Yes, we all get sparked at birth – or in fact even earlier, at conception. However, my birth was quite unique. When my mom was at her six-month pregnancy checkup, they noticed I was under distress. They immediately rushed her in for an emergency cesarean section. During this process, my lungs collapsed within utero and I died three times. As the medical team fought hard to keep me alive, they had to rush me to another hospital. At the time, the hospital where I was delivered did not have the type of neonatal intensive care unit that I required. Therefore, I did not see my parents for a few days' time. I remained in the intensive care unit on breathing machines and feeding tubes for a few months before I was able to come home.

Later on in life, through the amazing work of CranioSacral Therapy, I was able to recall this trauma and release the charges and stories I had developed around it. Even further, I was able to submerse myself in what occurred when I had died. The body is amazing and has cellular memory holding onto all the events that occur in our life. During this death experience, I was in pure bliss. I had witnessed large, star-like individuals that beamed with beauty. Within this realm, there were no genders, no races, and no labels like the ones that separate us here in this third-dimension reality. Here in this bliss, there was complete unity at the ultimate sense of the word. Each star-like being worked in harmony with the others. Even though there were no labels amongst them, you could differentiate each one as they each had their own unique sparkle.

Wow. I did not want to come back from this place. However, I chose life. I chose to come back to embody exactly that – to embody that bright beautiful light that we all are at our unique

9

core essence. As a result of this experience, I truly believe that as one shines his/her light, others will light up, too.

Prior to discovering CranioSacral Therapy, I had a few life events that assisted in the unfolding of my awakening and helped me to remember who I really was. As a child, I was always sensitive to the feelings and energy around me, not necessarily understanding what it was. I would easily cry and have my feelings hurt. This was very difficult for others to understand, especially my father. My father grew up very differently; in his world, you did not show emotions like this. He had a playful side at times but was also very strict with rules. This was an interesting contrast for me to witness and explore while growing up. Simply being a boy came with certain ideals and restrictions. One of these included not showing your emotions so that you could be strong. What a conflict that was to someone who was very sensitive.

Fast-forward a few years. I had just graduated college, finished my internships, and started my first job as an occupational therapist at Children's Hospital of Michigan. I was beyond excited; I was following my passion and loved what I did. During this short time, my mom had found out she had liver cancer. I was twenty-four years old. I was still young and naïve, believing that she would beat this and that life would go on. She opted not to do treatments, but to have a surgery instead to remove the cancerous part of the liver. I will never forget that day. Following the surgery, the doctor came out to talk with us and told us that when he was in there, they realized it was more than they had anticipated. They did what they could, but the outlook was not good.

Within a week after the surgery, my mom continued to decline and had to be admitted back to the hospital. The doctor called us all in for a family meeting – another day that I will never forget. He told us that her body was beginning to show signs of shutting down, and that she most likely would only have two or three days left. Remember, up to this point, I was still not fully comprehending (or wanting to comprehend) what was about to happen. That was my body's protective mechanism. However, in that moment, it was like reality came and kicked me in the face. *What?* I only had two or three days left with my mom. I couldn't even imagine this idea. My life was just beginning with my new career, and now this.

I slept in the hospital the last two days of her life. On the day that she passed, my sisters, my dad, my aunt and uncle, and I were around her bed, counting and watching her respiration fall to less than three breaths per minute. My brother-in-law came in and tried to change the television as he wanted to see some sport program; however, the channel would not change. He unplugged the TV and plugged it back in, played with the batteries in the remote, but nothing worked so he finally walked away from it. That is, nothing worked until my mom took her last breath. As she exhaled her last breath, the TV program that was playing turned fuzzy, and then the sports program turned on. We were all in amazement at that moment. It was her way of showing us that she was crossing over – a moment that would be the start of my new awakening. I thought to myself, *"If her spirit can do that, then what else is out there?"* It sparked such a deep place of inquiry within my soul. This place of curiosity would eventually lead me to where I am today. I will be forever grateful for the gift my mom gave me in her passing. Thank you, Mom.

Even though this sparked me so deeply at the moment, I was not in the place to fully awaken to my gifts. I went through a deep grieving process over the next year. The experience of losing my mother at such a young age flipped my reality upside down. What I had imagined and thought to be real was no longer. It was like developing a whole new story and routine again; one without my mom in it physically. Most of my friends were supportive, but they could not comprehend what I was experiencing as I was the first in this situation. I was relating to people much older than myself, as they were the ones losing their parents.

Following her loss, I went through what I call my "sex, drugs, and rock-n-roll" phase. I could barely fathom the pain and was blindly looking for ways to numb it to some extent, not realizing what I was doing at the time. This ties back to my childhood and the masculine role of not expressing your feelings and emotions. With my highly sensitive nature, however, that was (once again) not an option for me. I felt things within my being that I had never experienced before.

One does a lot of self-exploration when grieving such a deep loss. I began to understand that life was not constant. I saw how things can be altered so easily and so quickly. I was reaching new depths within myself and developing understandings that I had longed for. Her death altered me in ways I never knew were possible. I even developed a whole new relationship with my dad, as her loss shifted him as well. It was refreshing to know my dad on a new level.

Four years following my mom's death, I found myself back in a similar situation. My dad, who was very active and rode his bike every day, could no longer do so because his hip was bothering him. He was not one to take medication or go to the doctor. However, after a few months of being in so much pain that he could barely even walk, he knew it was time. He needed a hip replacement. I thought to myself, *I know many people who have had hip replacements and are doing great.* I had also worked with adults with hip replacements.

The day came for the surgery. When my oldest sister, Renee, picked him up that day, he told her where all his paperwork was in case something happened. He knew. The surgery went well, and he moved to recovery – that is, all was well until two days after the operation. Then he began to vomit a black substance, which they told us could be normal after a surgery. However, he did not stop. He also began to bloat. He eventually ended up in the cardiac unit, as the bloating was putting pressure on his heart. He had several doctors now on his team trying to understand what was happening. The primary doctor told him that he wanted to do an exploratory surgery to see what was happening inside because he could not continue on in such a bloated and distended state. It was leading to many secondary problems.

Therefore, my dad went in for yet another surgery, barely a week after the first one. The doctor came out and told us that he did not see anything wrong inside. This was good news, but still confusing since it meant that we did not know what was causing all this. He said he manually massaged and released all the air from the colon and put it in drainage tubes so that this would not occur again. Two days later, they told us he was doing better and that they were going to move him to step-down ICU. That night, however, we got a phone call telling us that he had taken a turn for the worse. It was a phone call that I will never forget. I flew as fast as I could to the hospital and met all my sisters there. Once we were all there, they came out to tell us that he had passed away. *"What?"* I thought to myself. *"How could this be happening again?"* I lost my mom four years ago, and now my dad. I had just developed a new beautiful relationship with him.

We wanted answers, so we had an independent autopsy done. The guy who did the autopsy told us that he does not often give families this advice, but that he strongly encouraged us to pursue legal action. When my dad died, two-thirds of his blood was pooled in his abdomen. He died from internal bleeding as a result of being on blood thinners that are known to cause this serious side effect. There were multiple documentations on his chart that he was showing signs of distress and internal bleeding far before his death even occurred.

We did pursue legal action, as we did not want this to happen to another family. It took over two years before the hospital settled out of court. During this process, I learned about the corruption that can exist within an organization, even in a hospital. They flagged his chart to the executives' office on the day he died, they omitted some of his chart when the lawyers requested it, and they dragged the suit out over two years, hoping that through the agony we would drop the case. We persisted, stayed strong, and ended up finding out that they settled to say (off the record) that they were in error.

Going through all this at age twenty-eight, I was completely upside down. Not only was I dealing with the death of my dad, but also with the corruption that occurs. I had more peace over my dad's death, as I knew he was with my mom. The two of them were reunited. However, my sisters were still upset and not sure if he had crossed completely.

One of my sisters, Colleen, won a raffle for a psychic reading. Since one of the options was to do a crossover for a loved one, we all agreed that we would come together and do this at my parents' house to make sure my dad had crossed and was doing well. So there we sat, all in a circle around the table in my parents' kitchen. My older two sisters were bit more apprehensive, as they were not as open to this kind of stuff as Colleen and I were at the time.

Once the ceremony began, I immediately saw my mom's and dad's energy beings. They were both smiling and happy. To know for sure that they were doing great made me feel so much joy. The medium turned to my sister and told her that my parents wanted to say congratulations on the new house. This comment caught my sister by surprise, since she had not told anyone yet that they were going to build a new house. After the ceremony ended, the medium guided us back. I opened my eyes I saw that I was physically in the room; however, I sure did not feel like it. I had never experienced this sensation before. I felt so light, free, and expansive. I could see my physical body, but I did not feel as if I were in it. The medium knew what was happening and explained that I was still between worlds. She guided me even deeper into a grounding exercise. Wow! This sensation was amazing. This would be yet another spark on my path. If I could see my parents' spirit energies and go to these other realms, what else was possible? It felt so easy to go there, and so natural.

I loved the sensation that I had felt. How could I achieve this state again?

Shortly after this experience, Colleen and I attended a psychic class over multiple weeks, exploring different avenues. One of the main things that each medium shared was that we all have gifts, and that we can all access this information. They also shared that one way to access your gifts and these other realms was through meditation. Therefore, I looked into different ways of meditation. I will always remember the day I sat down in my family room to try meditation for the first time. I did everything the book said – I lit the candles, created the sacred space, and got into posture. I have to laugh now, as while this is one way to meditate, meditation is more a way of life becoming a way of being. However, as I shut my eyes at that time, I was transported to another dimension. I could not even feel myself sitting on the couch. I felt as if I were flying. It was light and bright and free. Time did not exist. I felt so expansive in this state of being. To this day, I have no idea how long I was there. All I know is that I had experienced something within myself that I wanted to continue to explore. I wanted to feel like this all the time. It was a natural high. I had explored with many drugs in the past, but this was beyond that. This was a place I could reach on my own without the use of anything else. It was a place of beauty and peace.

I wanted to share this with everyone. Everyone should know how to do this and experience such a state. However, I soon realized that we are all on our own paths. I can only shine my light the way I know how. We all have multiple ways of getting to the same point. This is how my path was unfolding. I give my dad gratitude for the gifts he gave me in his death. Thank you, Dad.

I continued to explore and learn different ways of meditation. Ultimately, this led me to alternative healing methods as well. The case for my dad had come to an end. I had just turned thirty years old. One morning, I woke up and could barely get out of

15

bed. My joints hurt so badly that even the touch of the sheets brushing on my skin caused pain. All I could do was lay in bed and remain as still as I could. After two days, I had to see a doctor. The doctor did blood tests and found that I had the signs of the onset of an autoimmune disorder, with symptoms very similar to fibromyalgia. I immediately began to think to myself, *"I am only thirty. This is not going to happen to me. I am not going to live my life like this. I am going to change my story."*

I remembered I had a referral to a CranioSacral Therapist, and I decided to call her and make an appointment. I was desperate. After my first session, I got off the table and felt as if I could run a marathon. I had so much energy surging through my body. I thought to myself, *"This is how I'm supposed to feel all the time?"* This was my body's true essence. I had felt this in a meditation before, but now I knew that it was possible with this gentle bodywork. This sparked something in me – I wanted to know how to do this amazing work. As life would have it, there was a level one class coming to my area in two weeks.

The therapist also gave me a referral to a holistic doctor, so I went and saw Dr. Gren. He was like a scientist, with herb bottles and remedies all over his office. This was something new to me, but I liked it. I told him what was going on, and he tested my body's systems to see what I needed. As soon as he put the right bottles on my body, my body would jump or buzz with an electrical energy current. I was amazed. How could placing a bottle of herbs on me do such a thing? I was on my path of self-discovery and learning new ways to work with my body.

I never had another episode of fibromyalgia again. In less than a year of with working with Dr. Gren and getting CranioSacral Therapy treatments, my blood tests came back normal. I learned, though the work of CranioSacral Therapy, that my body had adopted a story. According to the story, I would develop an autoimmune disorder when I turned thirty, just like the rest of my family. As each of my family members turned thirty, they had experienced something similar. However, I did not know that I was running this subconscious story. When I found this out, I changed that story to one of health and wellness. It was my first insight into understanding that "genetics" are simply a story – a story of our past, our ancestors, and how we think we are. How many times do you say, "It runs in the family," "My mom/dad had it so it doesn't surprise me that I have it," or "We have poor family genes"? Yes, these are the thoughts and patterns that create your reality. Once we become aware of this, we can take control and put ourselves back in the driver's seat.

After my first session of CranioSacral Therapy and then taking the first class, I was immediately a believer in the work and the power of the body to heal. There is such an innate wisdom and intelligence within each of us. We just have to allow ourselves the possibility to tap into that again and listen. This began my journey of taking many classes to work with the body, mind, and spirit in such a different and unique way. I feel blessed to have had that experience, as it was a catapult on my journey of self-discovery. When I became an open receiver to the possibilities, life presented new options for me. As we shift, life continually shifts around us.

As I continued to explore meditation, bodywork, self-healing, and alternative medicine, I felt as if I were finally at home within myself. These all made sense to me. I had found the path that was right for me. Through these avenues, many new doors opened and unfolded yet more new discoveries. All I knew is that I did not want to turn back from this new path I was embarking on. Where I was heading, I was unsure. However, I knew I had touched a place that so many long for. The curiosity that I had known well as a young child was back again. I began looking at things with a new perspective and a new outlook. I realized that being highly sensitive was a gift to cherish within myself, not something to shut down or be ashamed of just because others did not understand it. I found a new strength within being vulnerable – within simply being me.

These were the main sparks that ignited my path of continued awakening. I feel honored to be able to learn and explore each new day. I wake up with the wonder what I will learn that day. The magic of life is in each of us.

2

The Great Pyramids of Egypt
John's Awakening Moment

This chapter is a continuation from my other book, *"The Process: Soul's Journey to Oneness."* I ended that book with a discussion of how I was being guided to travel for a different purpose. The first destination of new purpose was Egypt. Now I know I was being guided here so that I could meet John Moreschi, Jr.

It was December of 2009. A dear friend of mine, Anthony, called me and told me that he had just watched a movie that had reminded him of me, titled *"The Secret."* He mentioned that during this movie, they said a lot of things that he has heard me say over the course of the years.

He was excited about it and wanted me to watch it. Within a month's time, he came over to my house and we watched the movie together. When the movie came to an end, I had a huge smile on my face and tears in my eyes. This is what I had been going through – encouraging others and starting myself on the power of thought and manifestation.

It was all coming together full circle. Through this movie, I was able to witness other individuals, like myself, who held and felt the same beliefs. They further described the power and law of attraction. This is what I had been experiencing and sharing with others for years. It was so exciting for me to witness a whole community of speakers on this topic.

Inside the movie packet, there was an advertisement for one of the speakers, Mike Dooley. The advertisement included a link to his website, so I decided I would check it out. While browsing through his website, I saw that he had a trip to Egypt coming up in three months. I thought to myself, *"How cool would it be to go*

19

on a trip of this nature with like-minded people?" I was co-creating this event to meet the beginning of my spirit family.

Some of my old blocking patterns and beliefs began to arise. Some of those included: *"That is a lot of money to spend on a trip," "I don't have that kind of money," "Egypt is far away and in a country that can experience problems," "I do not know of anyone that would go with me, and I can't go by myself."*

However, I was quickly able to identify those patterns as old beliefs. I was able to allow them to come into my thoughts and then pass by without attaching to them or giving them energy. I knew I was ready for this trip. There was something inside of me that had a strong urge to go. This was that familiar sensation that had come up before. It was my inner guide and divine truth.

I called the number and found that there were still openings left. I followed my inner wisdom and booked the trip. I was going to Egypt in two months. I had only seen Mike Dooley in the movie. I knew from his website that he had written some books, but all I really knew was that I was supposed to go to Egypt. I originally thought my reason for the trip was to meet Mike and to listen to his presentations. I would soon realize that I was going there for an entirely different purpose.

The time was fast approaching for me to embark on my journey to Egypt. My family and friends were nervous, but excited for me as well. Many wanted to come, but their stories had other purposes. This would be the first trip that I would go on by myself without knowing anyone at my destination. However, I found comfort in knowing that there was going to be a large group of like-minded people there. The planning process alone allowed me to grow leaps and bounds – traveling abroad by myself (with a group of people I did not know), simply trusting in my inner divine self.

In March of 2010, I flew from Michigan to New York to get my connecting flight. At New York, I met some other people from the group. I immediately made connections with the people at the airport that were traveling in the same group. This confirmed my belief that I was on the right path and eased any worries I might have still had.

As people walked by me in the airplane during the flight, I wondered to myself if they were in the group too. I ended up sitting next to a beautiful couple that was in another tour group, also going to Egypt. We shared stories and life experiences during most of the flight there.

Once we arrived in Egypt, our group was so large that we were divided into two buses: bus A and bus B. I, along with my spirit family that I would soon meet, ended up on bus B. Together, we had co-created this amazing moment in time, all the way down to being on the same bus so we could connect even more deeply.

When we arrived at the hotel that first day, we had a few minutes to rest before meeting as a group for an introduction. It felt surreal to be in Egypt with a group of people that shared my perspective on life. Immediately, I was able to engage in conversation with others on the beauty and magic of life. I went for a walk along the riverfront with an individual named John Moreschi. I felt a connection with John and the knowing of familiarity immediately, even though we had just met.

The next morning, our adventures began by starting to tour Egypt. Over the next ten days, I would begin to understand the depths and lifetimes I had shared with John. This was one of the reasons I had been guided to Egypt – to reconnect with John and do meditations and healings with him and others in this sacred land.

While in Cairo, we visited the museum that houses King Tut's remains. I found it fascinating to actually see the history of something that occurred so long ago. Not only was I able to see this history, but I was also beginning to feel the energy of the land – a sensation that was a new experience for me at that point.

During my previous travels with my friends, I had experienced the beauty and sights of the various areas we visited. I had an appreciation for the history that had occurred, however was unaware that I was experiencing it on another level. During those travels, I did not realize that I could feel the energy of a land and what had happened there. I was experiencing that feeling but was consciously unaware of it within my body.

Egypt provided that opportunity for growth. I became aware of the strong energy that was present. I was able to feel the energy of the past. I was on a journey I would never forget – a journey that would shift me in yet another direction.

While in Cairo, we were also going to be able to visit the pyramids and the Sphinx. Of the connections I had already made, Hope informed me that Vilma and Candace were interested in doing a meditation at the pyramids. I was super excited to hear about this. I loved doing meditations, and what better place to do one than at a pyramid? This was the beginning of our soul family coming together.

We arrived at the pyramids. Hope, Vilma, and I climbed up to a ledge. We all placed our hands on the pyramid to feel and sense its energy. It immediately felt as if the pyramid was vibrating. I wanted to jump up and down with joy. I could feel the energy within this amazing structure. I was speechless. The three of us then held hands and did a meditation. Again, I felt as if I were going to fly away. The energy around us was so light, so free, and so beautiful.

Next, we were allowed to go inside one of the pyramids. We had to duck down and crouch to get inside. Before I knew it, we were standing directly in the middle of the pyramid. This was the vortex point of the energy in which this pyramid was built. There were approximately ten of us inside at the moment. We immediately came together as one, and Candace and Vilma led us in a meditation. The energy began to whip around the circle faster than I could imagine. I felt a surge of energy go through my entire body. I again was left speechless. It was such a beautiful moment in time.

Lastly, our group made its way over to the Sphinx. I immediately fell in love as we approached this area. The Sphinx radiated such a serene, loving, and playful energy. Since we had a large group, we had been given special permission to actually go down by his paws. I ran over to him and gave him a big hug. I was in pure bliss. This was very different energy from what the pyramids were radiating. I was completely amazed at how easily I could identify the different vibrations.

The Sphinx was the protector of the pyramids. He was very large in size. However, he emitted such playful and kind energy. I did not want to leave. I wanted to stay with the Sphinx. We were able to take a group photo next to the Sphinx, for which I was very grateful.

This journey was shaping up beyond words of expression. I was meeting and connecting with so many beautiful souls. I was experiencing energy like I had never felt before. I was living my dreams of co-creations.

Not only was I experiencing and feeling this strongly within my soul, but I was also capturing it within my pictures. I began to see white circular images in the background of my pictures, called "orbs." Each orb had its own unique shape and design within the middle of it. When the photos were enlarged, you could see gorgeous patterns of energy within the orbs. My belief is that orbs are amazing spiritual energy that is around us at all times, expressing that oneness. They may include spirits, relatives, angels, and guides.

As the trip progressed, the orbs began to change in shape and color. It appeared as if my camera was taking aura photography. I was so excited to be able to capture this amazing energy in my pictures, and I shared them with the entire group. Out of a group of more than sixty people, there were only four or five of us that had energy in our pictures.

Some individuals, being more skeptical, originally stated that it was my camera or that it was broken. To test their theory, I began to take pictures with my phone as well. To their surprise, the pictures on my phone captured the same energy and orbs.

I have one picture in particular that I especially treasure. We were about to go to a light show experience, when I felt the energy shift within me. Goosebumps ran all over my body, even though it was ninety degrees outside. At that exact moment, I knew to take a picture over the crowd. Even to my surprise, the orb appeared as if it were a "mummy." There was a small head radiating light that appeared very clearly in the picture, along with a body that was wrapped up as a mummy would be. This image was in between two random individuals. This orb was definitely a spirit that was present and allowed me to see it, for which I am very thankful.

Why was I getting these orbs in most of my pictures, and other people were not? I believe it is because I was fully open to the experience and appreciated the beauty of the energy. We are all pure energy at our most basic forms; therefore, life and death coexist simultaneously within the flow of life. Orbs are energy of people that have passed, but still coexist with us. I understood and acknowledged this principle.

Because I continued to get so many orbs in my pictures, I was given the nickname "orb guy." This is a name I hold proudly. Following this trip, I went back through the many albums I had put together over the course of the years. To my surprise, I found that I had been capturing orbs in my pictures several years prior, without any awareness at the time. There were often several orbs during family gatherings and parties at my house. I knew this had to be my mom, dad, and ancestors. This was another loving way of them showing me that they were still around.

The next leg of our trip was a five-day Nile cruise. Along this cruise, we stopped each day to visit more sights that Egypt had to offer. Egypt has many structures and temples, and I was thrilled for the opportunity to bask in their beauty.

By this time in the trip, when I would enter the bus, people would often yell out my name. I would go along and give people high fives and hugs. We were creating a bond that would unite us for eternity. I was beginning to acknowledge my own beauty and allowing my light to shine.

The morning that we embarked on our trip to the Valley of the Kings is a day that I will never forget. That morning, my new friends kept saying, "You do not look like yourself today. Are you alright?" I heard this from several people as we ate breakfast before we left the ship for the day. I felt "off" that morning. I was dragging and my energy was low. I felt as if my head was congested and body was achy. As we were getting ready, I had the initial concern that I might be starting to get sick. If I got sick in Egypt, what would I do? However, I quickly allowed myself to just be in this space with no energetic attachment.

I had no clue on what was about to happen for me. We entered the bus and set off for the Valley of the Kings. I tried to rest my eyes on the bus, which was unlike me. I was often full of energy and buzzing around.

We arrived at our destination. The Valley of the Kings is a place where they buried many of the kings and leaders in previous times. It had giant monuments, each of which had been built by a king in preparation for his death. They had a guard to watch over this area to protect it from outsiders and looters. They valued their kings and leaders, even in their deaths. I eventually learned that this area was looted and attacked on occasion by people who were searching for the gold and treasures buried with the kings. Was this the energy I was picking up on?

We visited two memorial sites, and the feeling within me felt as if it were growing. What was happening to me? Why did I feel so horrible? What was I processing? When we were standing in line for King Ramesses VI, it all finally made sense. I was about the tenth person in line, waiting for my turn to enter the long corridor leading to his memorial. I felt as if I were going to explode.

Suddenly, I had an intense feeling of sadness come over me. I immediately began to cry. Why was I crying? Where was all this sadness coming from? Why does it feel so familiar in this place? My friends Candace, Sara, and Janice were right by my side. They supported me as I began to cry even harder while we walked through the entrance and down the long hallway to his tomb. We traversed five long corridors before we reached the burial chamber.

At this point, Candace introduced me to the divine heart coherence meditation, a meditation to which I dedicate much gratitude and many blessings. It allowed me to come back into coherence with my divine self and observe the energy for what it was, even as I was being pulled into it so strongly. This place and energy felt so familiar. I knew other people and visitors around me were probably wondering what was happening to me, but at that point I did not care. I was consumed with the energy around me. It felt as if it had overtaken me.

I completed the divine heart coherence meditation while walking to the tomb sobbing, and I was able to pull myself out of the energy to some degree. It freed me up enough to make it through the rest of the tomb. The feeling that was coming up felt very similar to when I had buried my mom and dad. It was an overwhelming sense of loss and sadness.

When I finally reached the vault in which the king was buried, I had the sensation that I was related to him in a previous lifetime. He was family. I felt as if he were my brother. I continued to cry as I walked away from the tomb back up towards the exit. As I was leaving the monument, the guard gently smiled at me and gave me a hug. He whispered, "Thank you," into my ear. He understood what I was experiencing. I was not just another visitor; I had felt the energy of this area.

I felt a huge sigh of relief as I walked back out into the open air and sunlight. My dear soul family all came over and gave me hugs, one at a time. Their support and love were so overwhelming, it made me cry all over again. I thought, *"These are individuals I have only just met, but they are supporting me beyond belief."* It still brings warmth to me as I write this.

I had never experienced anything like that moment before, especially not to the degree to which it occurred. I had experienced past lives before, but only during a CranioSacral Therapy session – never in the type of setting in which it occurred that day. This brought another depth to the meaning.

Later, when I returned home, I felt compelled to research and see what the tomb of King Ramesses VI was all about. I had never heard of him up before. The information I found showed that his tomb, along with the decorations and scripts on the walls, tells the story of the origins of the heavens, the earth, and the creation of the sun, light, and life itself. This was all making sense now. This information felt so familiar, as it was another part of me learning about the transitions and flow of life – oneness.

As the group moved forward to the next tomb, I had to take a few minutes to process what just occurred. Again, I had the support and love of my soul family by my side, checking on me throughout the day. I had further experiences throughout the day, but nothing as extreme as what had occurred in King Ramesses VI's memorial.

This was what my body had been prepping me for during the morning. The feeling of being unwell was a sign that my body was bringing up something for release – a big release, at that. I am thankful that I co-created this event to allow for my soul family to be there with me, as some other people around did not understand what was really occurring. They were confused, as their blocking belief systems had never allowed them to witness this before. They had no clue what to do, what to say, or how to support me. Witnessing all sides was part of my process – to witness how people responded according to their blocks.

That night when we made it back to the ship, I only ate a small portion at dinner. Some friends were going up to the upper deck to hang out and asked if I wanted to join, but after the strong emotional day I had, I decided to go back to my room to rest and get some sleep. I had no idea that the day was not over just yet.

During the middle of the night, I had a vision that there was a ceremony going on outside my door. In the ceremony, people were carrying someone deceased and honoring his life. I could hear them talking. I immediately awoke from a dead sleep. I was surprised to find that my sheets were drenched in sweat. I ran to the door to see if I could see anyone or hear anything, but there was nothing there. This was just the completion of my process. It was allowing closure for what I had experienced earlier in the day. Since it was only three o'clock in the morning, I cleared off my sheets and went back to bed.

The next day, I awoke still in awe of what had happened the day before and during the night. However, I felt completely different. I had my energy back and felt like my true self again, but something had shifted within me.

When I left Egypt, I knew I would stay connected with my soul brother, John. Over the past several years, our paths have indeed continued to cross in New York, Oregon, and Siem Reap, Cambodia. Our lives seem to parallel each other at various points.

John has an adventurous spirit and follows his heart. I honor his individuality and passion to empower others by living his truth. I feel blessed that our paths continue to intertwine through life.

***

Here is John's awakening moment:

Look inside yourself and go deep within. Literally take inventory of what is happening in your mind and body, because once you start to identify the aspects of truly knowing yourself, then your entire exterior experience will change.

Greetings, fellow seekers! The name that was given to me when I incarnated for this lifetime is John Moreschi, Jr. I am a solo traveler through the jungles of time and space. I came here to learn, experience, and prosper! My journey has been epic, and continues to unfold in a manner of my own co-creation. The journey has been filled with twists and turns, along with excitement and wonder! I have earned a Bachelor of Science in Hospitality Administration and a Master of Science in Education whilst on my quest. These degrees have led me to work with some of the finest companies and with some of the most eclectic beings. More importantly, they have helped me on the path to self-realization and enlightenment.

Throughout my life, I've been exposed to a variety of belief systems, from Christianity and Catholicism to Hinduism and Buddhism. I've made a pilgrimage to Jerusalem, as well as to Tibet. I consider myself a universal being in more ways than one. I believe in the universe and our God-given right to co-create with it.

I grew up in a humble neighborhood of Bronx, New York. I am the son of a medical assistant and a construction worker. As a child, I was moved to many areas, which essentially became the fuel for my exploratory nature. I grew up confused with so many unanswered questions, and my questions were often silenced. As I have grown spiritually, I have learned to question everything until I receive answers that make sense and resonate with me. At a young age, I was led to the society of Las Vegas, where I received an excellent education in both hospitality and life. I lived among the wealthy and those who would do anything to succeed. I lived a materialistic lifestyle that the majority of our world strives to attain – fast cars, big homes, money, fame, and status. I could get anything and be invited into the most exclusive gatherings. In many ways, I had "made it."

Some say I had it all, or did I?

This arduous path would end with me giving up an elite lifestyle so I could return to my roots and embark on the spiritual journey. I was hollow inside, with very little substance. The glitz and glamour were necessary for me to discover the deeper mysteries of life, but it is the lessons of the journey that have "made me" qualified to write the chapter you are reading.

This is the point where I ask you to ask yourself, what is self-realization?

The way it was explained to me is that when we are self-realized, we become like gods. What that means is we understand that God created man in its own image. We are God manifesting itself, as individuals, in a collective consciousness. Upon realizing this, well, our worlds are never quite the same. With a life-altering visit to India, and another visit to the pyramids of Teotihuacan in Mexico, I would begin to comprehend the idea of self-realization and the nature of our true self.

With regards to enlightenment, I am constantly learning to reach this most auspicious state of existence. Enlightenment is a mystery, and that is the beauty of it. Through the practice of meditation, experience, and self-knowledge, I am gaining the tools to open its treasure. I have been blessed to have wonderful teachers who have presented themselves, when I was ready, to peel back the layers of enlightenment.

I consider myself a global citizen as a result of the travels I have endured in my lifetime. I am also a spiritual being, having a physical experience in this earthly dimension. My journey has taken me across the globe to far-off places one can only dream of going. The journey has instilled inspiration and confidence to continually explore the dynamic universe we are so blessed to be alive in!

I invite you to join this ride of ultimate adventure!

FOR WE ARE ONE!

And, the sooner we embrace that simple ideology, the better off we all will be.

In 2008, the "shift" or awakening would occur for me. I was led down the spiritual rabbit hole to an Incan Shaman in the heavens of Peru. It was there that I experienced who and what we truly are. I learned about Pachamama and Viracocha. Through an Ayahuasca ceremony in the jungles of the Amazon, the truth was revealed to me. My awakening would take place, and I would be fortunate to be initiated into a very special group of individuals from all corners of the world. The experience would expand my consciousness to see our world in a very different manner. Machu Picchu will forever be a gateway to pass into the portals of spirituality. I have been among a variety of teachers, gurus, and cultures ever since.

After my Peruvian rite of passage, I would be brought to Egypt to experience something even more spectacular with like-minded individuals from all across the planet. We were fortunate to go inside the middle pyramid, and I was privileged to have a very special moment as my group departed the king's chamber. My experience was a profound glimpse into how we can transcend. Transcendence is something that goes beyond the normal or physical level, and I will leave it at that! It was a life-changing event, and something that fascinates me to this very day.

After Egypt, my life trajectory really took off. I would go on to visit all Seven Continents and all Seven Wonders of the New World. A few years later, I would proceed in completing a thirty-two-mile trek around Mt Kailash in Tibet. The messages I received as I circled the symbolic center of the universe were both elevating and enlightening.

Understanding that we are all connected, and a part of a collective consciousness is illuminating. Functioning in a world that does not realize this concept can, at times, be challenging. But, I have answered the call to do the inner work and help bring others along. That is the reason I am writing this chapter today. Sharing knowledge and insight so others may better their circumstances is awesome! Spreading love and light is also necessary in this time of uncertainty.

Meditation has become a daily ritual and provides a profound effect on our wellbeing and inner peace. Higher levels of consciousness can be achieved through the meditation medium. Meditation is a natural, organic, and cleansing practice. It allows the meditator to reach samadhi or a great union.

I am the author of "Dream Mechanics: A Practical Guide to Creating Your Reality." In my book, I unveil thirty-four epiphanies I have realized on my personal journey. The epiphanies are crafted to help others tap into their internal guidance system. Following our inner guidance and listening to our Higher Self is a process, but once mastered, it offers life-altering results.

I am eternal. And so are you! We are made of the same stuff as the stars. Our physical manifestations are a product of our thoughts, and we co-create our reality with the universe. The benefits that come from living mindfully are immense, and when we cultivate our minds to be still, we live healthier lives. The spark of awakening can happen at any moment if you are open to its magic. My awakening has led to an unfolding of life that people dream of because I have learned to let go. Detachment is at the root of the awakening process and is the catalyst for its continuation.

I leave you with the message that whatever you are searching for, or whatever has brought you to this moment in time, remember that the answers you seek lie within. The door has opened for you. Remember to stay in the moment. Frequently ask yourself, "Who am I?" The veil will be lifted the more you do this, and more of life's magic will be revealed to you.

3

The Pyramids of Teotihuacan, Mexico
Nishant's Awakening Moment

When I came back from Egypt, my heart was full and expansive. A new life was unfolding in front of me. I had trusted in my divine truth and had been guided to meet such beautiful souls. In addition to John, another amazing star I met in Egypt was Atma Arani. We shared such a special connection while at the temple of Sekhmet. We were both guided into a separate chamber outside of where most of the tourists were. Inside this chamber was an etched carving of Sekhmet on the wall. Atma Arani and I joined hands and placed our opposite hands on the wall so that they connected to the carving of Sekhmet's hands. As soon as we connected this circle, there was an instantaneous surge of energy that strongly zapped around in a circle within us. I had never experienced anything like this before – it was truly remarkable. It allowed us to open to our hearts even more deeply.

Atma Arani and I kept in contact after our return from Egypt in March of 2010. In June of that same year, she mentioned that she was going to go to Mexico in two months to a place called Teotihuacan for a workshop with Don Miguel Ruiz and his sons. She said he was the author of *The Four Agreements*. Again, I had never heard of this place or these people before, but I felt this strong feeling arise within me – the same one that I had felt before going to Egypt. Therefore, I knew to trust this guidance and decided to book the trip.

In August of 2010, I was on a plane to meet Atma Arani at the Pyramid of the Sun and Moon in Teotihuacan Mexico, known as the "City of Gods." Her plane was scheduled to arrive before mine. I went through customs in Mexico with four other people whom were also attending the workshop, and there was a van awaiting our arrival. One of those individuals on the van was

Nishant. I sat next to him on the ride there, which lasted a few hours. We had an instant connection, as if we were brothers. Nishant and I talked about our personal journeys and how we were each guided to Teotihuacan.

He was guided there because he had read the book *The Four Agreements* and wanted to meet Don Miguel in person. Nishant was shocked that I had never heard of him or the book until just before this trip. We were both guided to this place in different ways to reconnect.

Over the next few days of the workshop, as we dove deeper into our own personal work, our friendship continued to grow even stronger. I began to realize that this is why I was guided to this amazing area – to do deep personal work and form a connection with Nishant.

Teotihuacan holds a very special energy within its grounds, ancient pyramids, and Toltec wisdom. We were able to do special personal ceremonies each day around the energies that support it on the Pyramid of the Sun, the Pyramid of the Moon, and the Avenue of the Dead (the structure that connects the two pyramids).

As we left Mexico, I knew I would be seeing Nishant again, trusting in the divine guidance that would once again draw us to one another when the time was right. Nishant and I kept in close contact with each other, calling often and supporting each other as we both continued growing and learning on this path of awakening. I love and honor our deep conversations we have had (and continue to have) regarding life, energy, spirituality, and existence. Nishant and I came together many more times, in New York and eventually also in Peru at the sacred site of Machu Picchu.

Nishant offers such a calm and gentle nature. He is able to view all perspectives in a conversation, which allows for deep growth. I honor Nishant, as he is dedicated to self-discovery and improvement on a daily basis – as am I. I am grateful our paths continue to cross throughout lifetimes.

***

Here is Nishant's awakening moment:

My name is Nishant. I live in Queens, New York, where I was born and raised. My parents came to America from India in the late 60s and 70s, and I am of Indian descent. I discovered in my mid-twenties that the origin of my name was from Sanskrit, meaning "the ending of the darkness of knowledge." I was surprised to discover this particular meaning, as this was the essence of my gradual journey towards awakening. I often wondered that when people speak about this term awakening, if we all are talking about the same thing. I hear it often used flippantly as if the person just bought a new pair of shoes. So that you, the reader, are clear, I thought I would define what I mean by it. "Awakening" simply refers to "waking up." This means that somehow I have been asleep, but this doesn't make sense at first. "I get up, go to work, school, job, and deal with family and relationships. What do you mean 'I am asleep?'" Well, we are asleep because we have identified who we are and whom others are based on "thought" or "knowledge." The journey of awakening, in essence, is the discovery of who we are beyond the conceptual mind, and the discovery of who others are beyond our story about them. Awakening is actually a destructive process – it is a breaking down of all that we know and hold dear as our identities. It is sometimes liberating, but often can be uncomfortable. It's a waking up to who we are beyond the story of who we are. Our names, nationalities, gender, ideas, and concepts of who we are... these are all borrowed as we grow up in our particular culture, families, and country of origin. Yet is that who we truly are? Is that what I am... just a story? Or am I something beyond it? Many traditions point to who we truly are with words such as consciousness, spirit, awareness, formless presence, Being, or the Self. Whatever term you want to use, for me, it just means "Who am I without my story?" This includes my story about my family, friends, society, and even myself. We, as humanity, have identified with our thinking mind for centuries, and it can create immense

35

suffering to the point where the joy and simplicity of being alive gets hampered down. I wasn't looking to awaken at all... I just wanted to know one thing... why do we humans suffer? And how can I end it? That was the spark towards a journey full of gratitude, joy, harmony, pain, frustration, terror, and inevitably a peace that surpasses understanding.

My journey really begins many years ago, when I came home after finishing my third year at my university. That summer, I unexpectedly started developing symptoms. I was nauseous, vomiting, my heart was racing out of my chest, and my stomach felt twisted in knots. Eventually, after going in and out of the hospital and getting tests done that came out negative, a psychiatrist walked into the hospital room I was staying in. He said to me that since the tests came out all negative, what I was experiencing were psychosomatic symptoms, and that I had clinical depression along with severe anxiety, hence the heart beating out of my chest. At first, I couldn't understand it; I was smart, I had financial support from family, I had a muscular body at the time, I had friends, but yet I was experiencing deep emotional pain. Then shortly one day after that visit from the psychiatrist, I lay on my couch at home, feeling paralyzed. I couldn't move due to the numbness of the emotional pain I was experiencing. I had thoughts of ending my life, and I was a bit shocked since that was the first time I experienced serious thoughts like that. Then, as I lay there feeling paralyzed, something of a faint whisper came to me from deep within and it said, "There is something you don't know," and then shortly after... it said, "and most of humanity doesn't know either." I don't know why or how, but I trusted this voice, and this led me to search for answers as to why we humans suffer. I decided to engage in psychotherapy and that supported in giving me a place to vent, but it wasn't getting to the root of the issue. I often wondered that if I go through relationship troubles or lose a job or something happens on the external level, does that mean I have to suffer and see a therapist for the rest of my life? So I looked to the only place I knew to look for answers... books. I read tons of books on ways to deal with suffering from human psychology, positive thinking, mantra meditation, motivational work, general topics on suffering, and inevitably spirituality. I didn't consciously go into it, but I was being guided by life to certain teachers that supported me in awakening to the Truth. What comes following are three of the main realizations I have had that led to my gradual awakening. Of course, I can write a whole book on the contributions of the people and various realizations I have had, but for the sake of this chapter, I will boil it down to three main important realizations that revolutionized my existence and where they came from that supported the awakening within.

The real beginning of waking up came from reading the work of spiritual teacher Don Miguel Ruiz. This is where I met the founder of this book, Rob Fournier, in Mexico, at a retreat with Don Miguel Ruiz. Don Miguel comes from the Toltec Tradition, which supports beings all over the world in recognizing that we are all "artists of the spirit." Through his particular book, "The Voice of Knowledge," I came to discover a very important mind-blowing realization which would transform my life forever. This realization was that "I, as a human being, when I look out through my eyes, I don't see the world as it is... I see my story about it." Before this realization, since I was asleep to the nature of the human mind, I thought that the voice in my head was "me." I thought that what my mind said about others and myself was truth or reality. I didn't know thoughts were just simply thoughts, and that part of being human with a mind is that the mind hands us lies that can "feel" true. I didn't know that it was important to change my own relationship to the voice in my head... that actually that was the most important relationship I could have in life, because that is the filter I see all other relationships out of. That the voice in my head was full of "stories" — not truths – that I believed in and picked up based on the conditioning of my family origin, culture, society, and upbringing. It was odd at first to think that our own minds are the source of suffering. Typically, I thought it was mom, dad, sibling, body issues, money issues, friend issues, or school issues that led to the pain and suffering I experienced. I wasn't self-aware; I was asleep. Then, with the support of Don Miguel, I really recognized that it is the story I am believing about others and life that creates my suffering, and that I can wake up from the story and discover it for what it is... a lie, not the truth. Unfortunately, or fortunately, this discovery was just the beginning. I tried not believing my own mind

37

when it handed me thoughts that I could sense were lies, but it didn't work. I still was over-reactive in relationships and would regret it after knowing that it was my own mind's story that led to my emotional reaction. The pangs of suffering, though loosened by this newfound awareness, still felt strong about things long ago and the future yet to come. That is where the Grace of the universe came in and offered me the most powerful tool I have ever come across in my journey, the Work of Byron Katie.

Although I'd had a significant realization that when I looked out through my eyes, I see "my story" about it and that is the cause of my suffering, it wasn't enough. I ended up heading back to the only place I knew to look... the bookstore. I stumbled upon the books of this woman named Byron Katie. I knew nothing about her, but as I read through her books, I noticed she had a method known as inquiry. Through her method, she supported herself and others to question the thoughts that ran through our minds. The questions include meditatively asking oneself on paper, "Is it true? Can I absolutely know that it's true? How do I react when I believe this thought? Who would I be, in that same situation, without that thought?" This step is followed by a process called "the turnarounds." For more information, you can go to www.thework.com. I came to the fascinating realization that, with the support of her method, I could question my story and help my innermost being wake up from the trance of thought. The more and more I sincerely applied her method for the love of truth, I began to experience more inner peace and less reactivity in my life. To be honest, it was hard after a while to find an apparent problem in the world once doing inquiry for some time, which is strange to even fathom as a possibility in the human experience. This was because I questioned what I believed about the world and woke up to the truth. I learned that it was my mind's argument with reality that caused me to suffer, and that I could question any story that would oppose "what is" and wake up to my heart's nature as Truth. With the support of inquiry, the journey of awakening was a gradual unwinding of the long-held, cherished stories I had about my father, brother, mother, body, money, and relationships. The whole range of human emotions, from humility to joy to discomfort to sadness to nausea, came up as I unwound story by story that created my suffering. It was the Truth that set me free, but I had to be open to discover what the Truth was, rather than being right. The ultimate choice: "Do I want to be right, or do I want to be free?" With the support of Byron Katie, her books, and also going to her events, I found the possibility of living a life of clarity, freedom, and inner peace no matter what happens. I am not saying this is easy... I am just sharing that this actually became a real possibility in my life experience and is to this day. It took hard work and still can be humbling, but now I know what the sages mean when they say the Wisdom is within. I didn't know how to access that wisdom within, I only knew to turn to books, but with the guidance of self-inquiry, I genuinely found it for myself within. I found a way home to my own innermost Self, which was further enhanced by my immersion in the Advaita Vedanta/Zen traditions.

The third important realization on my journey I came upon was from the Advaita Vedanta and Zen traditions. Once again, through my readings, I stumbled upon these traditions through various teachers and noticed they were asking the similar question of "Who am I without my story?" but asking it from a much deeper level of what we are, in essence, in this apparent existence. The realization that these traditions brought forth within me was that what I am is Pure Awareness or Formless Presence. In conjunction with the Work of Byron Katie, I came to a deeper understanding of what was meant when asked the question "Who am I without my story?" These traditions helped me dive into the depths of my being and come to the realization that the question to answer is not "Who am I?" in this thing called life, but "What am I?" What dawned upon me was the recognition that even when I am not "thinking" myself into existence... I exist... but as what...? When taking the inward path and noticing that I, as a human being, experience thoughts, images, feelings, sensations, and the five senses... the dive inward invites the question, "What notices all of these things?" When one dives into the heart of experience, one may discover, as I did, that there is a formless empty presence that is witness to the ever-changing fluctuation of thoughts, images, feelings, and sense perceptions. That what we are is this constant, whole, untouched witness, and the experience of that is that of being a Formless Presence. Not a person, but a presence. The particular person with a particular identity that we take ourselves to be is only relatively true in the world of form as we engage with others in society and is based on the mind but is inherently false and untrue when checking our inward experience. We are Pure Awareness or Formless Presence embodied in this particular body-mind. So the question "Who am I without my story?" is one that can go to the heart of existence and the core of what we are. Teachers such as Adyashanti, Eckhart Tolle, Mooji, and Rupert Spira have lighted the way towards this recognition for me and still serve those beings in which the dawn of awakening is permeating through their existence. This recognition of my true nature is a continual recognition and is firmly establishing itself as my lived experience in this thing called Life. Certainly, I get caught up in old habits or patterns of conditioning and more core stories of who I am are beginning to unravel, but what I can say to be true based on experience is that I am not the identity I took on at birth, and this is continuing to unravel in my life experience more and more.

So, what now? What's left? If I have come to the realization that what I see is a story when I look out through my eyes, that I can question this story for the love of truth and I can recognize that what I am is Pure Awareness or Formless Presence, then what is left on my journey? I am only thirty-two years old at the date of this writing, so what's left? The answer to that question is the Embodiment of what has been realized. For some on the awakening path, I hear they have a sudden awakening and then it is done for them. For me, awakening is more like a slow crawl. I am like the turtle in the race with the rabbit. There is nowhere to go and no one to become. This kind of a life can be unsettling at first and disorienting, but eventually some sense of inner balance pervades my existence. The continual recognition of my true nature and the continual questioning of my own mind all support one thing ultimately… the Heart to shine more brightly no matter the experience on the outside. Most people are searching to get what they want to be happy. I have given up that search mostly. I am looking for something more profound. Can I be FREE even if I don't get what I want in this lifetime? The only way I know how is to continue to Keep Waking Up and move towards those parts of me that are not yet Awake to the Truth within.

In my daily life, I entered the profession of being a psychotherapist where I serve my clients in waking up and raising awareness of the trance their own minds puts them in, and how their own minds create their immense suffering. Sure, clients come in with all sorts of issues, but the source is the same… what story are they telling that keeps them suffering and prevents them from shining more brightly in their lives. Sometimes this is met with resistance, because the ego-mind is more interested in being right than free. But for those that are open to another way, I serve in offering the Work of Byron Katie and various other meditative practices as a therapist to help in waking up to the heart. This is done by seeing who we are without our story. Clarity, freedom, and inner peace are our birthrights, and there is only once place I have discovered that those things exist… within the Wisdom of a Questioned Mind and the Discovery of who we are beyond thought. If I were to give it a name… perhaps I would call it… Love.

4

Himalayan Mountains, India
Vikas' Awakening Moment

When I got home from Teotihuacan, Mexico, I sat in my family room in amazement. In a short six-month time period, I had embarked on two journeys that allowed me much greater expansion. I was smiling ear-to-ear at how beautifully life was unfolding in front of my eyes. I soon began to realize that I was traveling for a different purpose – a purpose that was guiding me to my highest potential and for the good of greater consciousness. This felt so different, yet so right. Where would I go next? The last two places had come about so quickly and effortlessly.

In December of that same year, 2010, I was having dinner with a friend, Shannon. We were having an enlightening conversation about life, energy, and following your guidance. I mentioned to her that I had a deep desire to go to India, as I had been studying meditation, yoga, and alternative medicine for some time. I felt this calling deep inside to go there, as I wanted to give back as a way of gratitude for the gifts that came from the culture. However, things were not aligned just yet, since I did not want to just go and tour around. She shared with me her experience of volunteering abroad and doing her student teaching in England. As soon as I heard these words, I knew that was it! Being able to volunteer in India was the missing link. My body was buzzing with energy. I knew this feeling and recognized it as a big sign telling me that it was the right thing to do. I had not thought of volunteering abroad before.

I got home late that night – after 1:00 AM – and was still excited beyond belief over this idea. Therefore, I sat at my computer and started searching for volunteer options. I did not know where to begin, so I pulled up Google and simply typed in "volunteer in India." To my surprise, there were multiple options and websites that came up from the search. Wow – how was I going to pick amongst all these options? I started at the top of the list and clicked on each website link so I could read about the company. After checking four different sites, with the clock reading even later now, I thought to myself, *"I should go to bed and look again tomorrow."* However, I clicked on one more site – the fifth one in the search. It was called "VolunteerInIndia.com." As soon as the webpage pulled up, I started crying hysterically for fifteen minutes. It was a moment of pure joy beyond anything I had experienced before. How could just opening a webpage create such a reaction within me? I believe it is because it was in direct alignment with where I was being guided next. After I wiped away the many tears, I took the time to actually read through the site. It was in complete harmony with what I wanted. I knew by the reaction I had that this was where I was going and that it was the exact right place for me.

There were options on this site to volunteer to teach English to children, to teach English to monks, and to participate in community outreach programs in various locations around India. One of the sites was Dharamsala. I did not know where this was in India or the significance of this town, but knew it was calling me there – as I read this town's name, I had another reaction of my cells buzzing. As I looked it up, I saw it was the town of his holiness the Dalai Lama and the many Tibetan monks who were exiled from Tibet, China. I was astonished by how I had been guided to this site. Not only could I volunteer in India, but I could do so with the Tibetan culture as well as the Indian culture. This was like the best of both worlds to me.

However, as I again read through the volunteer options of teaching English or participating in community outreach, something was not in full alignment just yet. What was this missing link that I was feeling? Everything else was showing me that this was exactly the right company and exactly the right town, so what was missing? As I sat there for a few moments in meditation, it came to me. As a pediatric occupational therapist and craniosacral therapist, I felt as if I had my own unique gift I wanted to offer to India. Therefore, I reached out to the company and let them know exactly what I did in the States to see if it was possible to utilize my skills with them. I figured, *"Why not?"* I had to try and see, since that is what I felt was in alignment with what I needed to do.

They got back to me the next day, and I was amazed by their response. They appeared to be just as excited as I was. They told me they had just opened a school in Dharamsala for children with special needs about a year prior. They had two special education teachers working there, but no therapists yet. This is why I felt the urge to reach out to them and offer a different volunteer option. Things were coming together so easily and perfectly. This was all happening in January of 2011.

Another beautiful option that they offered was to tour India to different sites for two weeks prior to starting the volunteer work, as well as the opportunity to do different weekend trips during my stay. My dream was coming true. I would have the opportunity to explore India and give back by volunteering. The company put me in direct correspondence with their guide and host in Dharamsala, Vikas Nehria. I would be doing a home stay and living with him and his family. Little did I know at the time that this is another reason why I was being guided there – to meet Vikas and his family. I would become lifelong friends and brothers with Vikas.

I was working at a school district at the time, but I had summers off. Therefore, I planned to go to India and volunteer during my time off in July and August, which would give me two months there. This allowed five months to plan, obtain my visa, and get all my things in order. Yes, I was still in the phase of my traveling days when I would prepare and plan to go somewhere. That makes me laugh even as I write this – now, several years later, I do things on whims and when I get inspired, I go.

This would be the longest stretch of time that I had ever lived outside the States. I did not know what to expect, but I did know that I was beyond excited and that everything was lining up so easily and perfectly. A month before I left, I even came across two separate individuals that had just returned from medical volunteering in India. They gave me insights and supplement ideas to bring, especially for travelers' diarrhea. This came in handy later, when I experienced what they call "Delhi belly." However, there was one particular piece of wisdom one of them shared with me that I still remember to this day, and it was beyond helpful. She told me that since I was intuitive and sensitive to the feelings of areas around me, and also since I did meditations, I needed to be aware of my own state of consciousness while there. She explained that the land of India has a tendency to magnify things energetically, even more than the States, and that the effect is almost immediate. If you were thinking and feeling in a positive manner, for example, more of that would come and your days would flow easily. However, if you were experiencing anger, frustration, or anxiety, that would also magnify quickly. This magnification is helpful either way, as it becomes a very large mirror so that you may see what you are projecting into the world and be able to shift into your true divine self.

In July of 2011, the time finally came. Some family and friends were nervous about me living in India for two months, but I knew this was where I needed to be. On the long flight there, I sat next to a guy from India who was doing work in the States. We got into some amazing conversations about healing, spirituality, and life. I even did a little CranioSacral Therapy with him right there on the plane. When we landed, he guided me through the airport and customs. He even emailed me the next day, telling me he shared our whole conversation with his wife and invited me to stay with them. I was on another plan, unfortunately, but we stayed in touch. This would soon be an almost daily occurrence – having beautiful conversations about life and spirituality, sharing meals with strangers, and experiencing a sense of community everywhere I went. I knew I loved India before I left, but I love India even more now.

After almost twenty-four hours of travel, I embarked on the drive from the airport to New Delhi where I was going to stay for four nights so that I could explore the area. The traffic in New Dehli was unlike anything I had ever experienced before. There were four-lane highways, but instead of four cars (one in each lane), there were five cars, three to four motorbikes, and sometimes a cow – not to mention horns beeping everywhere. Someone once told me that they summed it up as "organized chaos," and that is exactly what it appeared to be. It was especially chaotic to me, coming from such an organized sense of being in the States; however, there was a certain flow that worked within this new system I was witnessing. It was fascinating and mind-blowing at the same time. Over time, I would become even more amazed by the beauty of how everything flows in India – even the traffic.

I made it safely to my hotel and found it to be very stylish. The owner immediately came over as I checked in and told me that he had heard I did CranioSacral Therapy. I took my bags to my room and, within minutes, started doing CranioSacral Therapy on the owner. I had to chuckle at myself at the beauty of the moment. He was so grateful for the experience, as was I.

After exploring the many monuments, temples, and treasures of New Delhi, I took the train to Rishikesh. I was excited to go there, as this was the city of ashrams on the famous Ganges River. When I got off the train, I saw thousands of people. There just so happened to be a huge festival going on. It would normally have taken about an hour to get to the ashram where I was staying, but it ended up taking eight hours. The driver and guide kept apologizing, but I was laughing as I was enjoying the ambience of being in the middle of the festival. How wonderful to be submersed right into the culture. I was able to stay in an ashram for a few days and participate in some local ceremonies on the river. My last day here was particularly special. I went down to the Ganges River and did a meditation. While I was there, an elderly woman approached with a plate of flowers and ceremonial offerings. She did not speak English, nor did I speak

Hindu, but the interaction was priceless. She prepared two flower petals and allowed me to send them off along the river in honor of my mom and dad. This would be the start of me engaging in a local ceremonial tradition to honor my mom's and dad's spirits in each country I visited.

Next, I took an overnight train followed by a long car ride to reach Dharamsala and Upper Bhagsu. When I arrived, one of Vikas' dear friends greeted me and showed me to my room so that I could rest. I was exhausted. Later that day, Vikas came by to introduce himself and show me around. He was as vibrant in person as he was in correspondence. That night they had an opening ceremony to commemorate the grand opening of a new meditation hall located on their family property. I thought to myself, *"I am so lucky to be here on the day it opened."* Vikas knew I had a deep interest in meditation and allowed me to join the daily meditations in the hall during my whole stay. What a special added bonus! The meditations were a mix of Osho and tantric nature. I had never heard of Osho before I arrived there. I thoroughly enjoyed my time learning a new form of meditation, combining movement, sound, and vibration. One of the individuals who was with Osho during his time, Swami Chaitanya Keerti, and his partner Aprana, even lived directly above me in the guest house. It was so charming to be able to get to know both of them and share in some enlightening conversations.

The next morning, Vikas told me he had to go to the restaurant they owned. His mom and wife also both had to go into town, so he gave me his son Ibu, who was just a few months old, to watch for a few hours. I had to laugh inside, as this concept of leaving your child with someone you had just met was so different from the custom in the States. When I shared this story with him later, we both laughed and he said, "Well, you were family now." This is how I immediately fell in love with India. As soon as you meet an individual, you are instantly family. Wow, how that creates such a different way of being and sense of community. I felt so at home in this new country, as if I had always been there.

My first experience at Vikas' restaurant offered another beautiful example of the sense of community and different way to living in India. I arrived, found an open table, and sat down. Within seconds, two Indian men came over and asked if they could join me. I said, "Sure." They shared with me how in other countries, when entering a restaurant you would find a table that was empty and go sit by yourself. They said, "Here in India, when we enter a restaurant, we go and share a table with someone already there, as we are all family." It was definitely a new concept to me, but I loved it already.

Over the next two months, I became even closer with Vikas and his family. They were all so kind, welcoming, and generous. I got to know his wife Nisha, along with his mom, dad, and brother. I was invited to all family gatherings and ate my meals with them or in the family restaurant. Vikas took me to visit many temples, and we got to participate in many local Hindu traditions, which I loved.

Some of the weekend trips included visiting the Taj Mahal, the India and Pakistan border ceremony of changing of the guards, and Amritsar to visit the Golden Temple. Each one was unique and special in its own way. I felt truly blessed to be able to attend such sacred sites. The Dalai Lama was in town during my stay, doing a three-day teaching on loving compassion. I was fortunate to be able to attend his teachings right there, within his monastery and home. Following his teachings, I was even part of a special group of fifteen people that got to participate in a private question-and-answer session with him. This was like a dream come true. I had to almost pinch myself, to think I was sitting in India and with the Dalai Lama. This was just one of many magical moments on this adventure that took me by surprise.

Making my way each day from Upper Bhagsu down to the school where I was volunteering, Harmony Through Education,

48

was a journey like no other. From Upper Bhagsu, I would walk twenty minutes down the Himalayan mountainside along with the billy goats, cows, and oxen on my way to the town of McLeod Ganj. From there, I caught the public bus as I learned to squeeze my way on. Just as you would think that the bus was full and could no longer hold any more people, as everyone was standing literally chest-to-back with the next person, five more people would somehow find their way on. The bus would then take turns around the small mountain dirt lanes as I would watch with awe. After my twenty-minute exhilarating ride, I would hop off in Dharamsala and walk another twenty minutes through the city streets to the school entrance. Meeting the students and teachers at the school, Harmony Through Education, brought tears to my eyes. It was like witnessing my dreams coming true. Working with each of these students and the staff was such a special gift. The staff had such a passion to assist these students in reaching their fullest potentials and educating the community for integration. I am grateful to have been able to be a small part of that. They were so open and receptive to all new ideas. I was able to provide them with stretching and positioning programs for kids that had tight musculature, as well as sensory integration examples for kids with autism. I also modified equipment and came up with and built some new stuff for them. It really allowed me to expand my thinking outside of the box and become very creative with the materials that were available or ones that I could find in a store.

To my surprise, I happened to be in northern India during monsoon season. I had never experienced rain like this before. Wow – it rained nonstop for several days on end. To be honest, it was tough for me mentally, as I am a person who loves the warmer weather and sun. However, I learned that life still moves on, even in the torrential downpour of rain. You roll up your pants, put on your raincoat, and off you go. Umbrellas did not work so well in the winds. Since it was monsoon season, the school I was at had a monsoon break (instead of spring break like we have in the States) and was shut down for two weeks. This allowed me an opportunity to work with the Tibetan monks and community, teaching them English during my time off from the school. It was such a heartbreaking experience to listen to their stories of how they managed to escape the harsh conditions of China. This is when I learned a new level of deep compassion, and what it means to be truly compassionate. These individuals – even after all the heartache, rough conditions, and instances of watching some of their loved ones be murdered – had nothing but compassion and goodwill for China. Wow!! I have told this story to so many people. Could you have compassion for someone who killed your loved one? They explained to me that harboring or fostering hate and anger would hurt only them. It would also match the same energy of the person that caused the harm. Therefore, offering love and compassion broke the cycle and allowed for deep healing. This is the true meaning of the word "compassion."

My time in India was filled with so many beautiful life lessons, cherished moments, and the stripping away of old beliefs. One of those beliefs was all the material belongings I had. I lived from a small bag of clothing for two months and was happier than I had ever been. Living a simple life was rewarding and less distracting. The clutter we have around us, on our walls, and/or in our houses, truly does make a difference. Simple is better. This is only one of the lessons I integrated after leaving India. This experience in India was another huge turning point on my journey on self-awakening.

When I first came back to the states, I struggled for a while as I was processing and integrating all that I had learned and experienced. How could I bring back what I had learned and incorporate it into my life now? For example, when I went to a local store while in India, it was just a small room (very different from the large department stores we have in the States) and the owner/workers would engage in conversations with you about life, spirituality, energy, and so on – sometimes for hours. Usually, after your enlightening and stimulating conversation, they would offer for you to come over to their house to meet their family and share a meal. Therefore, coming back to the

States and going to a local store was not remotely the same. Here, the workers barely look up to say hello and definitely will not engage in conversation for more than a minute at a time, especially if it isn't work-related. However, over time, I made it a point to greet everyone in the store and try to engage them in conversation the best I could, bridging the gap between what we experience here and the beauty I had seen while traveling.

Over the years, I kept in contact with Vikas on a regular basis. He was my brother now. I came back to visit him and the family again in May of 2017. His town is a special place that truly feels like home. I know I will be back again to visit many more times to come.

Vikas has a spark about him that makes everyone feel at ease and at home. He is usually bursting with a smile or a laugh, enjoying each moment of life. Vikas has a huge heart, often looking for additional ways to support his community. He operates a tour company that is unique in that it combines both travel and spirituality, understanding that all is one. I feel blessed to have reconnected with Vikas again in this lifetime.

***

Here is Vikas' awakening moment:

Namaste. My name is Vikas Nehria. I am from Bhagsu Dharamsala, India. This place is in the Himalayan range. I live here with my family. I run my family business of a home-stay guest house and work as a tourist guide. As a tourist guide, I organize and help people explore India and what they can do here.

Born here in the Himalayan area, I feel blessed naturally. When I was growing up I saw lots of gatherings, compassion, and love in my village. I met so many masters and tourists all from different places. I had the opportunity to learn different culture, religion, and spiritual activities. As living in India and born in a Hindu family generally we are practicing Hindu religion, but my family we practice Shivism most. That is more praying to Lord Shiva and the goddess of the mountains and spirits.

As I met different people, I got connected with a different way of spirituality where I find that religion is same, which is trying to help peace and happiness to humanity. But when we realize above it, then we are thinking of spirituality, where all the religions are equal. You are thinking towards a connection of nature and humanity.

My awakening/awareness occurred in several steps. When I was sixteen, during those years, I met a couple of spiritual people. At that time, I was meditating and doing yoga. I realized that getting connected I had a special energy that I never felt before going through my body. This energy was something I cannot describe. After studying with them, I thought to leave my house and stay away. But then after process of thinking and debating with my mind, I realized that I should stay here with my family. I feel this I should live the family life. I feel I have some duties towards my family. I thought maybe I was here to have family experience. So I continued to study Masters of Tourism Management. During this time of my life, I continued with spirituality and my home life both.

This was a long-term decision. Everybody has this situation in their life where they have long-term decisions and short-term decisions. This was my long-term decision because I know what I decide at that moment would affect my whole life. So I was talking to myself, not only one day, but for a long, long time. Because I don't want to get trapped by my mind or the thoughts later on that the decision I took was not good. So, what happened? I realized that we get this life, so I was very young, and it was interesting to understand these kind of feelings. Maybe it was because I got in touch with the people who were very wise. After I realized that life is very important, and family life, staying in the society, taking care of your parents, and to live this life and be with the community. At the same time, you can practice yourself self-spirituality. You can make balance. This universe has given us opportunity to live the life to experience all the things within the community. See what is happening around you and live that life. It made me to think that I can be in the community and *live this life and share with the beautiful people around us. This made me to think to stay with the family.*

So of course, there was another thought in my mind to live outside this family and community I can get self-realization. But I choose my family life.

When I was twenty-one, my friend who I met during studies told me that they had some spirit issues going on in their house. They were doing some cleansing for this. One day, he came to me and asked me to come to the forest to throw something wrapped in a cloth. We went in the forest and threw that thing. We got on the scooter and started to drive away and I looked back. He then told me, "Don't look back." It was too late; I already did. I then became quiet and did not say anything to him. I did not know what was going to happen and I did not want to ask him.

After a few days, I met with an accident. I was on a bike and a cow jumped in front of me. For a few seconds, I was dead. This is a very special moment where two of my friends who were dead already pushed me back. Both friends were classmates of mine. One passed at fifteen years old, and the other at nineteen years old, from tragic accidents. They said, "It is not time for you." I still remember this so clearly every day. So, after this, I have realized there is something for me in this life. I made myself one beautiful line, "Live your life as you like." Here in my life, I want to live it as happy and make others happy.

As soon as my friends pushed my back, my eyes opened. There were local people who took me to a clinic, as I was far from home. At the clinic, I got my first aid. They called my friends and family. After a couple of hours my friends and family came and took me back to Dharamsala, which was more than two hundred kilometers away, to get better care. I was in the hospital for two weeks. My legs were injured, and my arm was broken. I had to have surgery on my arm with a metal plate put in.

I have only shared the story of my friends pushing me back with a few close friends up until this point. It is special to me. In this accident, the cow died. As you know, I am a Hindu, and this is a big thing that a cow died. So, my parents were told by the society that it is a bad thing, and you have to do some cleansing as well. So, they took me to Hardiwar where there is the holy river Ganga, a sacred place for Hindus. We performed some cleansing rituals for purification. But all the time, I was telling my parents that it was not my fault, it was the cow's fault. He jumped in front of me and was going to kill me. What I have thought from this accident, I need to be more calm. All things are related and connected.

After my studies, I came back to my family business. My mother then asked me to get married. First I said, "No," because I thought I was too young. I was twenty-three at the time. She kept on asking. I again talked to myself on what to do, as you know that when I was young, I had a conversation with myself that I would stay with my family. That made me to think more that what I have realized earlier that I would stay with my family and take care of them. But I was too young to get married and realized that if I marry now or a couple of years after, maybe there is a difference, but at that moment I decided that if my family is asking me to get married that they are right. For me also one special thought came that I can get married and have family life. This was the same thought from when I was sixteen of family life, so I knew it was true for me.

So, when I was asked to get married, it was a long-term decision. As my mom asked me many times, I realized she was missing something. I was the oldest, and I found that I had a duty to her and my family. I was thinking again and discussing in my mind another phase in my life. So I talked to myself again a long time and decided, "Okay, I will get married now." Again, maybe a few things hit me in my mind that we have this energy and capable to take care of kids/family. We have special energy in this age. This period of time we have to live family life. Also, I was believing that if I was here in this life, also there is something which has some kind of duty for me. My parents brought me here, so I have duty to bring new life to nature, these things click in my mind.

I have realized that maybe yes, it was time to get married and take care of my family. So I said okay to my mom. So they arranged my going to be wife. They arranged it through a family friend. I went to see her and talked to her. We met for a few times at lunch. I have realized that I can marry her. She said that she liked me and she would marry whoever her parents wanted. From the arrangement, she was the first I met and I was the first she met.

After my marriage of one year, we had our first son. He is now seven years old. I also have another son of two years old. It feels nice to play with them. So now I am living the decisions I made in my mind to have family.

Whatever my experiences are, I want to pass on/share with others. My life is going full of different people around the world. One special community that lives in Dharamsala is the Tibetan community. I have been getting connected with them over the years. I want to understand their life better outside of their country. It has always been a connection for me to be together with them and help them as well. Getting to know this community, it has helped me to be more strong as they live far away from their family and country and survive. So I feel like I made the right decision to stay with my family in this life. It made me to put love and compassion for others. This is what I learned also from people and would like to share with them as well.

5

Himalayan Mountains, India
Vijay's Awakening Moment

It was August of 2011. I had been in India for just over a month, and it had started to really feel like home. Every morning, I would wake up and join the meditation group at the hall next to the guest house. It was a beautiful way to start the day. Then I would get ready, eat breakfast, and begin my journey to the school where I was volunteering. The only exception is when they were closed for monsoon break, during which time I would instead head to Bhagsu to work with the Tibetan monks and their community, teaching English.

In the evenings, I would attend local events, hang out with friends I made, or simply go and listen to the Tibetan monks as they all gathered to do Gregorian chants (which was outstanding to witness and be part of). As this time, it was the start of monsoon and raining almost every day. I had developed a few colds due to the damp, rainy, cooler mountain weather. This led me to explore Ayurvedic medicine and treatments, ancient traditions that are powerful. I also became really good friends with the beautiful couple from Finland that was staying next to me at the guest house. They were there doing a cleanse and also attending the morning meditations. They had gotten a referral to a local Tibetan doctor that was hard to get into and invited me to join them. I graciously accepted. On the morning of the appointment, you had to bring with you your morning pee. When we arrived, we found the waiting room was packed with wall-to-wall people. We waited over an hour, and then our names were called. A stunning elderly Tibetan man, who had to be at least in his late eighties, asked us for our pee. He mixed it with something and disposed of it just as quickly – all within seconds. He asked about my symptoms, looked at my tongue, and wrote down a prescription. This took all of two or three minutes, at the most. I took it over to the counter, and the lady gave me what appeared to be brown pellets and told me to take them daily. She had given me a form of Tibetan herbal medicine. As soon as I got back home, I immediately took the herbal medicine. To my surprise, within a day's time, my symptoms of the sinus infection and the severe diarrhea that I was also experiencing completely started to clear up. I was astonished and amazed. This was another confirmation of the power of alternative and herbal medicine. I loved how it was simply part of the culture here – so widely accepted. This resonated so deeply with the work I was already doing. I feel so grateful for this experience.

One evening, I returned from an Ayurvedic sinus treatment massage called Shirodhara. I was hungry and headed to the family restaurant for dinner. When I arrived, Vikas was there and wanted to introduce me to his brother-in-law, Vijay. Vijay was in town visiting his sister, Nisha, and the family. Vijay was beaming with a bright light around him and had the best smile around. We became instant friends and brothers. I remember that night so vividly – we sat around the table for hours, talking about the beauty of life, energy that we are, spirituality, and everything in between. The conversation flowed so easily, as if I had known Vijay for lifetimes, which I feel I have. I was reconnecting with a member of my soul family. I knew this feeling from before, and as always, it brought joy and a smile to me.

Vijay was only in town for a few days, as he had to get back to school and work. However, because we were soul brothers coming back to reunite, we were able to visit, hang out, and connect on such a deep level, even in that short time. I am still in awe at the beauty of how things like this align… what a beautiful alignment that he chose to visit during my stay there, especially since I was only in India for a (relatively) short time. Even after Vijay left, we kept in close contact. We would often message each other inspirational quotes or messages of the day. Let me tell you

– those quotes always came at the perfect time. I feel very blessed to be able to reconnect with my brother again in this lifetime.

We met in August of 2011. Since then, we have stayed connected through messaging. I was guided to go back to India in May of 2017. I began this recent trip back to India in Dharamsala, visiting Vikas, Nisha, and their family for a few weeks. It was wonderful to reconnect and see all the changes in the town. It felt as if no time had passed. Vikas picked me up from the airport on the day I arrived, and by that evening we were attending a local wedding of one of their friends. The following week, I was even able to experience a celebration of life of a relative who passed. It was that immediate sense of family again. No matter how long it has been, an openness and welcoming is always there.

I knew Vijay had recently moved to southern India for work. Therefore, I booked a flight and flew down to Gujarati as I wanted to reconnect with him as well. Again, it was beyond amazing to reconnect in person with Vijay. We picked up right where we left off last time. The conversations we engaged in were (and are) so fulfilling to my soul. Vijay is such a kind, warm-hearted individual. During my weeklong stay with him, I got to meet and visit with all of his friends. He also took me to see the place where Gandhi did his march. Witnessing that part of history was fascinating.

I feel blessed to be able to have gone to India not once but twice, and to have been able to reconnect with my dear soul brother Vijay. Vijay is such a vibrant being of light. His natural essence emits a beauty all can see. I am grateful that we have and continue to stay connected. I look forward to the beautiful creations our future holds.

***

Here is Vijay's awakening moment:

Namaste (hello). My name is Vijay Totaniya. I am from Palampur, India. Presently, I am working as an assistant manager at a local bank in Navsari. Navsari is a town that is 1,666.6 km away from my hometown. My family consists of my mom, dad, elder sister, and younger brother.

I am from a Hindu family. I worship Lord Shiva. Lord Shiva is one of the principal deities of Hinduism. Shiva is the Supreme Being who creates, protects, and transforms the universe. I am from a shepherd family called Gaddi tribe. The Gaddi tribe lives in the Dhauladhar Valley. It is a very good culture. I love the songs and the festivals. In one of the festivals, we go round and round in circles as we dance to the tunes of music and drum. The most important thing of the tribe is the 25-yard long strand that is tied to their wrist both men and women, which serves as a symbol of tribe.

As my dad is working in the army, I am very fond of joining the Indian army. At the age of nine, there was a war between India and Pakistan. I saw dead bodies of soldiers coming back to their homes. This is the turning point of my life. My father is also in war at the time, and we were very tense. Every time we were watching TV, we were praying to God, please save my father.

By watching these conditions, when I was sitting alone something happened inside of me. I felt very enthusiastic and energetic. First time I talk with my inner soul. This was the first time I realized something inside of me, as I was very young and did not know exactly what it was. I came to know that I was not born to do the same as my family to work with animals in the fields.

I decided to join Indian army, but at that time I was very young boy. I was following that of my inner soul from when I was nine. So I started preparing for Indian army. I took first exam at the age of seventeen. I did not pass the exam on the first time. I was disappointed, but never lost hope. Again, I started to prepare for the

59

exam, and it took me four years to pass the first part. I cracked the exam at the age of twenty-one and cleared all of the four hurdles of physical and psychological, but the last hurdle I was not able to. The last hurdle was a conference in front of the Indian army in where they ask questions of all sorts. They then decide if they take you or not. They decided not to take me. I was very disappointed at this time, as I tried for years to get in. This was my spark that I thought.

Since I did not pass the last hurdle, I thought I had to move back home and do my ancestors' business. This business was one of shearing sheep, selling wool, and raising/selling goats. After completing my graduation at the age of twenty-two, I come back to home. But still I did not have any job to do. I had completed my btech degree in electronics and communication.

When I got home, I kept searching for a job but didn't get any. I was searching for two years and started to lose hope. I felt very depressed and would lose my confidence a lot. I hit a state of depression. I lost hope, interest, didn't want to buy any new things, didn't want to sing, didn't want to talk with people or hang out with friends, and felt like dying. I was a different person at that time.

I just finished university and people were asking my parents what I was doing and what job I had. But I had no answer. These questions pinched me a lot. After you finish school, it is thought you get a job. I could feel this in my parents. I was in a deep state of depression but still did not want my parents to see. This was very hard to me. This is the first time I am talking of the depression. I did not want my parents to worry about me. I felt I had to be happy in front of them. I did not share this depression with others as they would not understand.

In between I went to Chandigarh for searching of the job. One day I was sitting alone and doing Facebook, I found a school friend. Through Facebook we met, and after a few days I met with her. By watching my condition, she felt very sad. A person that is very jolly and entertainer was now very sad, so she started to cry at this. Then we started to share old school memories, and this made us very happy

60

again. I felt that she came into my life as a miracle. This was the first time I felt happy in long time.

Every day she called me in the morning and night. We started to spend time together. She slowly started to inspire me to do banking and the exams. At that time there was a boom for banking industry. But I still did not want to do anything. I heard a voice deep within me saying, "Time changes everything." I know now that this was the same of my inner soul talking to me when I was at the age of nine. However, I was struggling to listen to this voice as I was still depressed. With my inner voice and the inspiration of this girl was a turning point.

One day I was so depressed I started crying in front of her. I have never cried in front of anyone except my parents when I was young. By watching these conditions again, she tell me stories to inspire me. One story was of ants and it trying to climb a wall. One ant would fall many times from the wall but still ant would not lose hope. It would try again and again many times. I still remember this story today. It has a big impact on me. Here is the poem that I have saved and read. It is by Suryakant Tripathi Nirala:

*"The boat that qualms the waves
Never gets across
The mind that dreads and dares
Has never been at a loss
The tiny ant, when it carries the grain
Lays it up into the heights of the wall
Falls slipping a hundred times,
Just as it tries again
The faith in the mind
Stirs courage in the nerves
It soars and slips, then slips and soars again
Until its efforts have not been in vain
The diver who scrounges deep into the oceans
Comes bare in his fist a number of times*

61

It is not so painless
Each time he delves to hit upon a pearl
Someday, when out of those deep seas he whirls
And in surprise, that his efforts have brought
Glad, for his fist is not empty every time
And in him that seamless effort
Herald a cheery chime
O' accept the failures that cross our way
They are just the challenging mile stones
And build from right here, where you fell
Until all the shortcomings cease,
And your soar in success
Burn restful sleeps in the sacrificial pyres
Until tireless struggles brought smiles of joy
Oh! Do not run away from the battlefields
For triumph always yields such joy
Just after relentless endeavors.........."

This poem changed my life. I started to prepare for the banking exam with enthusiasm and with dedication. Luckily, I cracked the banking examination after six months. After cracking the examination, the old Vijay came back. This was soul. I again started talking with my inner soul and it said, "I am happy." I started to sing again, and all things come back on the track. This turning point is because of that girl and the poem she shared. I am very thankful for that. She will remain in my heart forever.

I started working for the bank at age of twenty-five. I have been with bank for two years now. I have learned to do whatever you are doing with your passion. You can see that I have changed with my passions. I started out with going in the Indian army and now I am in banking.

You have to listen to your inner soul when it is talking to you. Do whatever you want to do, but with passion and talking to your inner soul. Take time for yourself daily, about ten to twenty minutes. It will change your thinking power and how you make decisions. I take at least ten to twenty minutes each day for myself and meditate. During this meditation is when my soul talks to me.

When I listen and talk to my soul is when things go smoothly. Time changes everything.

6

Machu Picchu, Peru
Romulo's Awakening Moment

After living in India for two months, coming back to Michigan in September of 2011 was quite an adjustment. My first week back, I fell into a slight depression from the fast-paced lifestyle I was seeing again in the States. I missed walking down the Himalayan Mountains and, most importantly, the sense of community that was built into the culture. When I went to a local store in my neighborhood, I was not experiencing those deep life conversations and connections that occurred daily all over India. Most people were on a mission, had a list, and followed an agenda on what they were going to do next. It took me over a month to fully integrate back into the culture of where I was living – and even then, there was still a yearning of something missing.

I felt like leaving and going back to India right away. However, a friend of mine made a good point: "Maybe it's about bringing what you learned in India here." Yes, that felt right to me. My mission became bringing that sense of community to where I was, reaching out to people in the local stores even if they were not as receptive as people had been in India. I was always one to talk and start up conversations wherever I went, but this new perspective gave a deeper level to my mission.

I had also purchased several Tibetan singing bowls while in India, as I was fascinated with the sound vibration and how I felt when I heard them. I was excited to incorporate them into my CranioSacral Therapy work and at the schools with the kids. This was the beginning of my exploration of sound vibration and all the amazing effects it has on the human body. Later, this would lead me to creating weekly sound immersion sessions at our wellness center.

A few months passed and integrating was getting easier. One day, I was on the phone talking with my dear soul brother Nishant, whom I met in Teotihuacan, Mexico, from Chapter 3. I was always grateful for our wonderful conversations, as I would often glean insights from them into what was going on for me during times of transition. On this particular day, I was sharing with him all of my adventures in India. He has family descent there and was greatly interested in what I had to say. He then shared with me that he had been looking into going to Peru to visit Machu Picchu. Wow – as soon as he said this, my body went into the "buzz" state again. It was the state of calling my Higher Self to a certain area.

Therefore, over the next few days, Nishant and I both looked into various tours and companies to visit this ancient land and site of the Incas. Nishant's only wish was that if we went, he wanted to do the four-day trek along the Inca trail into Machu Picchu itself, rather than taking the van up to the sacred site. I was in agreement – if we were going to do this, I wanted to explore the ancient trail that the Incas used. However, with that said, I do have to admit that I was a bit hesitant; I read that the trek was not that easy, and I had never done anything like this before... but I trusted my higher guidance and went for the plunge.

We emailed a few companies and looked at different packages. We quickly realized that we would have to book as soon as possible, as the trail permits were already almost completely booked up for the next season. Nishant found a company called Peruvian Magic, with whom correspondence was easy and flowing. They had a last-minute opening for the season coming up, so we took it. We would be going to Peru in three months' time. This would be just enough time to start training and get our bodies ready for the trek. The company recommended that those who don't climb and trek regularly, like us at the time, train for a few months prior to the trip. Once we were on the trail, I definitely understood why they recommended the training.

Since we were going all the way to Peru, I got the guidance to also add on Easter Island. I knew that, at this point in time, I was traveling for a different reason and being guided to ancient ruins and lands for a higher purpose. Nishant agreed that after our time in Peru, we would visit the mysterious Moai statues of Easter Island. What a "double whammy" we were about to experience! We were ready... so we thought.

I was excited to be able to see Nishant again and to go on another adventure with him. What a perfect adventure to go on – traveling with a spirit brother to a spirit land. As I knew from going to India and Egypt, journeys like these can bring up a lot of emotional, physical, and spiritual clearings. Therefore, I was thrilled that we would share in this together and support each other along the way.

In April of 2012, it was time to head off to the land of Peru, followed by Easter Island. We arrived in Peru and got to our hotel to rest. We had a few days to explore the ancient ruins of the area and to acclimate to the altitude. This acclimation period was very important; they wanted us there a few days prior to the trek to allow our bodies to slowly adjust to the altitude.

We soon met our guide for our entire journey in Peru, Romulo. It was so amazing to meet him in person after all the email correspondence. He was such a delight in person, as he was through email. He welcomed us to his country and tailored the whole trip to our needs. On one of the first nights there, he had a local shaman he knew come do a ceremony with us. What a special treat that was to be in ceremony with a local Peruvian shaman! I had studied shamanism in the States, but to be here with a local guide doing a local ceremony was unbelievable.

I will never forget what Romulo said to Nishant and me on the day that we started off on the Inca trail. He told us that the trek we were embarking on was more than just a hike – it was journey. This journey would impact us not only physically, but also mentally and spiritually on all levels. He ensured us that he would support us in any way possible, on all levels. He said there may be days or times when we just need to be by ourselves while hiking, and that it would be okay – we would all meet up at checkpoints. Starting off the trek with these words meant more to me that he even knew at the time. This is why we were guided to Peru at this time, specifically with this company and with Romulo. He understood the depth and levels of what could transpire for people (and himself) beyond the physical aspect. I honor that in him.

I had no idea what I was about to explore within the depths of myself, but do we ever really know? Day one of the trek was astonishing. I had the wonder and excitement of a child. Romulo had told us that the first day's portion of the trail would be up and down, but the easiest day of the trek overall. We hiked for about eight hours, with a stop for lunch along the way. The scenery and views were just breathtaking. The energy demonstrated by the assistant guides we had with us was humbling, as they carried the food and gear, set up all meals and our camps, and, despite all that extra work, passed us along the trail. From a serious trekking standpoint, we had it easy – we only had our day packs to carry. I am very grateful for these individuals. This was one of my first long treks, and I would have never made it without their support. At that point, I struggled just trekking the trails each day.

Day two was called "up day." We were about to trek for nine or ten hours, straight up in elevation. As we hiked, it got colder and the air became less oxygenated. It reminded me of climbing stairs for ten hours. You know how you feel after climbing a few flights of stairs? This was like that, except that we kept at it all day long. We took many breaks to catch our breath and stretch our burning legs. Nishant struggled on this day, as his asthma was acting up. I remember him looking at me at one point, not knowing if he could make it. However, we were literally on the side of mountain with nowhere else to go. He took his moment that he needed and found his inner strength to carry on. I tried to encourage him the best I could that day, as it was indeed challenging. I remember Romulo saying to us that, in case of an emergency, the only way off the trail was a medi-evacuation by helicopter. I could understand this, as we were extremely remote.

Day three was called "down day." After all that climbing up we did yesterday, we were about to climb down it all now. It rained most of this day, which added another challenge to the trek. Surprise – this would be my day of challenge and deep emotional release. I love how this was beautifully orchestrated; Nishant had his moment the day before, and now today it was my turn. The steps we were climbing up and down were not even large enough for my feet... I guess the Inca had smaller feet. As a result, I often had to step sideways. I lost my footing a few times, since the rain made the surfaces of the steps slippery. After hours of having to continuously look down at my feet and paying close attention to where I was stepping, I could feel the anxiety build. I just wanted to look out and enjoy the scenery. I was afraid of falling and injuring myself, as some places the trail was very narrow and steep. About six hours into the ten-hour trek, I stopped alongside the mountain cliff. The emotional buildup at this point was simply too much. I sat there and cried for a good fifteen minutes, purging all kinds of emotions. I was releasing physically from the pain of trekking for the past three days, emotionally from the state of fear, and spiritually from the feelings of all who had passed before me on this path. I remembered what Romulo had said earlier and allowed myself to take my time and space on this day. I then regained my composure, as I knew I still had hours left to hike and it would get dark soon. I just wanted to turn that next corner to see our camp. Romulo was a great motivator, as he kept saying that we were almost there. This is when I found a new inner strength that I never knew existed – a strength that I would remember and recall in future moments in my life. When we finally did arrive at camp for the night, it was nightfall. We had been hiking for at least ten hours. I was exhausted on all levels.

On day four, we got up before the sunrise to trek to the beginning of Machu Picchu so that we could experience the sunrise there. I woke up with a new perspective, knowing it was our final trek. To witness the sunrise upon the ancient city on top of the mountain cliff was breathtaking. I sat there in meditation, reflecting on my journey to arrive here at this sacred site. What a journey it was. I took a moment to honor myself for making the trek, as well as all the individuals who supported me along the way. I was amazed by how this city was built and the energy that was present. I could not even believe it was real, that we had just trekked along the Inca trail and were now sitting in front of Machu Picchu. This is a part of history – a site with such a story to tell.

We then explored the chambers and rooms within the sacred site. I stopped again to do a few meditations in certain rooms that called to me. It was as if the point on top of this mountain cliff was an access point to higher dimensions, a communication portal. We were able to explore Machu Picchu the next day as well, after we got some much needed rest in a hotel room. However, it was interesting to observe that the journey along the four-day trek along the Inca trail had more of an impact than the actual destination itself. The site is outstanding and a special place, for sure, but we were both guided to do the Inca trial for a higher purpose; it propelled our higher selves forward by leaps and bounds. It challenged me physically, mentally, and spiritually to find new depths within my soul, for which I will be forever grateful.

After exploring a few more days around Peru, we headed off to Easter Island. Nishant was only able to spend one night, as he had to get back home. I stayed on for a weeks' time. Even to this day, I am still unsure of the energy that I experienced there that week. It felt as if I wanted to run off the island and leave with Nishant when he left. The Moai statues were very fascinating and intriguing, but the overall energy that I experienced at that time was unsettling. I went for hikes each day and spent time in meditation around the statues, but never received the clarity I was looking for about what I was feeling. I believe part of my lesson there involved being able to be in an energy that is not necessarily comfortable, but to stay centered within my own self and not to get lost within the whirlwind. This can be a very important skill. This was the clarity.

Overall, I'm blessed to have followed my inner guidance again and to have said yes to the opportunity of going to Peru with my spirit brother to connect with yet another divine soul, Romulo. It is beautiful and divine how we were led to the exact right place, at the exact right time, and to meet the exact right people. Romulo was the perfect guide for us on this journey through Peru. I love how he guides people through the ancient sites with the understanding that more is happening in and around us. His knowledge and inner ancient wisdom of knowing is remarkable. I will be forever grateful for this experience and meeting Romulo.

***

Here is Romulo's awakening moment:

Hola, mi nombre es (hello, my name is) Romulo Castilla. I am from Cusco, Peru. I am a professional tour guide (Spanish and English), have almost 40 years' experience in the tourism industry, worked in Cusco as a travel and tourism agent, tour leader, and with a five-star hotel. In addition to tourism, my background also includes extensive studies in anthropology.

I have my own travel company, PERUVIANM MAGIC JOURNEYS, for more than thirteen years; I lead and guide spiritual groups to all Peru and Bolivia. We offer custom tours and journeys for individuals and groups (small or large). My expertise as tour guide is the Inca spiritualism, esotericism, and mysticism.

I studied various healing modalities of alternative medicine that utilizes energy with methods and techniques to boost the immune system, enhancing the body's innate healing ability as:

- Reconnection/Reconnective Healing - Levels I - II - III - Dr. Eric Pearl

- Body Talk Healing Modules I - II - Don Ka'imi Pilipovich

- Pranic Healing

• YOUR HANDS CAN HEAL YOU WORKSHOP – Master Stephen Co.

• PRANIC HEALING Level I - Master Stephen Co.

• ADVANCED PRANIC HEALING Level II - Master Stephen Co.

• PRANIC PSYCHOTHERAPY Level III - Master Stephen Co.

• PRANIC CRYSTAL HEALING Level IV - Master Stephen Co.

Pranic Healing Higher Courses

• ARHATIC YOGA - Master Choa Kok Sui

• HIGHER CLAIRVOYANCE - Master Choa Kok Sui

• SPIRITUAL ESSENCE OF MAN - Master Choa Kok Sui

• KRIYASHAKTI - Master Choa Kok Sui

- Student of Ramtha's School of Enlightenment, the School of Ancient Wisdom.

I have a family. I am married with Giuliana, I have four beloved children, Rhona (34), Aaron (32), Navarreaux (11), and Frederic (9).

My awakening/spark moment happened when I was eighteen years old and went for many years; it was when I wanted to leave my body. This changed my life and I started to investigate more about it.

70

My body would start to paralyze completely. It would start from my feet and go all the way to my head. I was fully aware of what was going on. It was so scary I couldn't move a muscle of my body, nor speak.

I didn't know what was happening with me. In Cusco by that time, people didn't know much about spiritualism or other things in the invisible world, until I met a friend from Piura. She was a healer and explained to me that probably I wanted to leave my body. This experience went for years.

Then I got aware about my hands that were always hot and started to use them applying energy to heal myself if I had a pain or hurt any part of my body, and also use it with my kids and family members.

On the following years I learned a healing modality with my healer friend from Piura. Thereafter I moved to Los Angeles and started to study different other modalities since 2001.

I first studied The Reconnection Healing with Dr. Eric Pearl, and had what's called my personal Reconnection, and I think that is when as I say, I would start seeing life and things in a wider screen, understanding first about me and my body, what I am in reality and what I do on this plane of existence.

My healing abilities improved very much and also my studies, I would understand easily books that for many people would probably be difficult to understand or would take long time. My spiritual evolution was faster.

Then I studied Pranic healing. I did almost all the basic and higher courses with Master Choa Kok Sui and Stephen Co. I found Pranic Healing very simple and easy to use anywhere I was. As a tour guide, I had tours and hikes at high altitude in Cusco and other cities in Peru, and in many opportunities people from my groups got sick and even injured, so I was able to apply advanced Pranic Healing and within minutes they felt a lot better.

There was something missing in my life, and all what is the alternative or energy medicine, the last link of the chain was the

71

Ramtha School of Enlightenment. Studying there made me understand many things that were unclear, questions unanswered by philosophy, science, and religion. They addressed fundamental questions about human existence, our origins and destiny, and the nature of reality. How in reality, consciousness and energy creates the nature of reality.

I now know, we are all GODS.

My awakening made my life easier. I had a better life in all ways, inner peace and greater love with myself, always healthy, relationship with my wife and kids the best, financially well, was able to help other people.

Know that you are GOD and the power is within you. You can create the life and reality you want.

Love, Peace, and Joy.

Romulo Castilla

Professional Tour Guide

Advanced Pranic Healer

Reconnection Healer

Peruvian Magic Journeys

Email: romulo@peruvianmagic.com

Web site: www.peruvianmagic.com

Cell Phone in Peru: 011-51-984888954

H/O Phone in Peru: 011-51-84-268883

7

The Outback, Australia
Shane's Awakening Moment

In the summer of 2013, my niece, Miranda, was finishing up her degree in special education and trying to decide where to do her student teaching. One option that she was guided to was Australia. I mentioned to her that if she went to Australia, I would come visit her. I had always wanted to go there. Well, she picked Australia, so I was going to uphold my promise.

She was going to be there until April of 2014. I decided I would go visit her at the end of her studies so we could explore some of Australia together. When I had envisioned Australia before, there were three things that I really wanted to experience: the outback, the Great Barrier Reef, and Sydney. I started to explore options to see these either on my own, with a tour, or a "hop on, hop off" bus pass. I asked my niece what she would want to do when she finished her student teaching. She was not keen on the idea of camping in the outback but was interested in seeing the Great Barrier Reef. That made the decision easy for me – I would fly in two weeks earlier and do the outback by myself, and then meet her at the Great Barrier Reef.

I looked into options and tours that went into the outback. I came across one tour that was ten days long and covered the main highlights of the outback, including sunrise and sunset at Ayers Rock. They had one opening for the time I was wanting, so I booked it. When things flow easily and smoothly, I know it is the right decision. If I have to think about something and debate about it in my mind, it is an indicator that I should not be doing that option.

While my niece was doing her student teaching, we stayed in contact. She messaged me about how much she loved Australia and that she was thoroughly enjoying her time there. This made me even more excited to be there with her and finally make it to a place I had always wanted to visit.

Finally, the time came. At the end of March 2014, I flew on multiple planes to get from Detroit, Michigan, to Australia. After reaching Sydney, I took my fourth flight to connect to Adelaide. On this connecting flight, I was definitely tired and jet-lagged – I didn't even know what time of day it was. However, I sat next to the most amazing individual and we discussed the power of thought and healing your body. I shared with him about being a CranioSacral Therapist and did some work with him right there on the plane. He was a physician and was fascinated by the work. He said he was just beginning to realize the power between the two (thought and healing) versus being more traditional. Before I left the States, I brought three copies of the book I had just published *The Process: Soul's Journey to Oneness* with the intention of giving them away to individuals I felt guided to. Well, he became the first person I gave a book to. I love the divine intervention when you witness it unfolding.

Once I arrived in Adelaide, I had three days before my outback tour would leave. Therefore, I reached out to a friend, Erin, who lived in Adelaide. I had met her in an advanced CranioSacral Therapy class. She graciously allowed me to stay with her while in town. It was so great to reconnect and catch up. I was amazed that I was sitting in her house. After we left our class we of course stayed in touch, but I had no idea I would be sitting in her house a year later. I love the connections we make and how they intertwine throughout our lives.

A few days later, it was time to embark on our ten-day journey from Adelaide to Alice Springs. I had no idea what I was about to encounter, but I was excited for the adventure. I met our driver and guide, Shane. He came out with the most energetic smile and burst of energy I had ever seen. What good vibes! I knew immediately this was going to be a good time. He ran through a brief orientation and asked if we had any questions. I raised my hand and asked, "It said we were sleeping in swags;

what is a swag?" I learned it was an Australian term for an outdoor insulated sleeping bag with a small mat inside it, and that it had a flap to pull over your head if it started to rain. I had to laugh. Yes, I went into this adventure (as I do most of them) not fully knowing what I was about to embark on. I follow my guidance and intuition and when that is right, I know I am exactly where I need to be. The rest will all fall into place and I will find out what I need.

The group all piled into the outback truck, and off we went into the unknown. Our rough daily schedule for the adventure was as follows: have breakfast, pack up camp, drive for a few hours, do a hike, eat lunch, do another hike or drive a few more hours, set up camp, make dinner, and enjoy the campfire and stars. We would all become a very close group after ten days of camping, hiking, and traveling together. It was such a beautiful group of people from all around the globe – fascinating on how we all ended up in that same spot on that tour. We became like a family, all assisting each other and helping in the chores.

As the days went on, it was amazing to witness how Shane connected to each person individually. He had such a spark about him. He truly made each person feel important and seen. It was easily apparent how much Shane loved what he did. It was so refreshing and beautiful to watch someone follow their passion. It showed in all his actions, from the music he played, to the food he cooked, to the stories he shared. Through it all, he was genuine. I smile to this day just thinking of that time we shared in the outback. I truly believe a group leader can make or break a group, and he was out-of-this-world phenomenal – a true leader and soul in every sense of the word.

The swag was actually more comfortable than I had imagined. I really enjoyed each evening, clearing a space on the ground from sticks or rocks, unrolling my swag, and looking up to see the Milky Way galaxy above me. I had never seen the stars and universe quite like I did in the outback. It was outstanding, to say the least. Witnessing such beauty and pondering existence under the stars was a definite highlight.

The evening campfires were another highlight. We would all sit around the campfire, share stories, and Shane would play the guitar, or we would engage in some funny, silly games. I remember having some deep belly laughs over these new games we played. These are moments in life that I remember and cherish – sharing laughs and good times with other special souls.

We did have a bit of an adventure the first few days in the outback. It was our second night and it began to lightly rain, so we put the flaps on our swags up to cover our faces. Well, within a short fifteen minutes, it turned from a light rain into a heavy downpour. Shane guided us to all come together in a single row, as close as we could in our swags, and then he put an additional tarp over all of us before he climbed in. We huddled shoulder-to-shoulder, with a tarp directly on top of us, as the rain continuously poured for hours. At one point, we all started to laugh – this was certainly one way to get to know each other! Needless to say, I am not sure how much sleep any of us got that night.

The next day, it was still raining as we packed up camp. We did a small hike in the rain with all our rain gear on. That night it was still raining, so we were unable to find a remote place off the road and sleep in the outback itself. Instead, we found a camping site and slept under a picnic pavilion, on and under the picnic tables. The group was still holding strong and making the best of the adventure.

On day four, the rain still had not let up. At this point, Shane got some phone calls from headquarters. They told him about the strong weather conditions we were experiencing. They also told him that part of the outback roads were closed, as some trucks were getting stuck in the mud. This was in the direction we were supposed to be heading. This meant he had to come up with a new route and a new plan. Shane said this was definitely unusual weather – he had not seen rain like this in a long time.

So, we changed our plans, and that night we actually got to stay at the most unique lodging place I had ever seen. It was a hostel that was underground. We had to walk through rock tunnels to get in. It was so cool! Shane apologized, saying that they usually do not stay in hostels since this was an outback tour, but Mother Nature had a different plan for us. Our group was excited to stay in dry beds for a night and to experience this amazing place. Again, I am grateful for how things aligned to allow us this opportunity. I was blessed, as our group was phenomenal, and we had the best leader out there. Everyone stayed so flexible and adaptable.

The next morning, we started on our new route to drier lands. The rest of the trip ended up being sunny and beautiful. We got to see Ayers Rock at sunset and again for sunrise, which was magical. The outback is such a special place and holds a very unique energy.

As our trip came to an end, I gave Shane a copy of my book. He was the second person I was guided to give it to. I knew he was a special soul, and I knew that we would stay in contact. I'm so grateful that we were able to cross paths when we did.

Next, I was off to meet my niece at the Great Barrier Reef. I got there two days before she did, so I had time to enjoy a hot shower, a clean room, and a comfy bed after camping for ten days. It was great to reconnect with her and hear about the end of her student teaching. It almost felt surreal to be sitting with my niece in Australia, just like we had talked about months prior. Most boats were booked, but we found one to take us out. They even offered an introduction to scuba diving along with snorkeling – another thing I had always wanted to try. What an experience to try scuba diving in the Great Barrier Reef! However, I do have to say that with it being my first time and having only gotten a brief lesson on the boat ride out there, I was a bit nervous. I enjoyed the experience, but I knew that the next time I attempted scuba diving, I wanted more formal training so I could feel comfortable with the equipment.

It actually took me a day or two to recover from scuba diving, as I was experiencing vertigo. I now know that I probably descended or ascended too fast for my equilibrium. What a trip it was to sit at dinner with my niece and feel like I was still moving on the boat, not able to ground myself. Thankfully, the sensation subsided in about two days. We also found a place where you could interact with a koala, which was something on both Miranda's and my wish lists. It was out of this world to be able to hold a koala in my arms. They are so soft and beautiful. These were rescued koala's they said that were unable to be released back in the wild.

Our last stop was Sydney. Miranda had already been there with her classmates, so she showed me around to some of the sights. It was beautiful to be able to take a tour of the Sydney opera house and ride along the canals. What a charming city.

I am thankful for the unfolding of events that guided me to Australia and to meet Shane. Shane holds such an amazing presence. He displays natural leadership qualities, truly appreciates the beauties and simplicities of life, and embodies a sense of joy.

The story of Shane's awakening moment is a bit different than the others'…

As I discussed earlier in the introduction, sharing and writing your personal journey can bring up a lot of feelings and emotions. These feelings and emotions can become blockages to writing, causing you to question your beliefs and the importance of your story. Further, it can lead to old patterns of coming up with excuses that prevent you from sharing. It can be easier to tell yourself that you are simply too busy or do not have time than it is to share your deep personal beliefs with others. These patterns can be subconscious, without you even being aware that you are doing it.

I feel that it is important to discuss this, as it can be a very common thread a lot of us share, one that we are working on becoming more aware of. When I was guided to meet these men from all over the world, they openly shared their stories with me, and I with them. We were in the present moment, supporting space for each other. However, as time passes, and we move out of that in-the-moment space, old patterns and beliefs can then arise.

Even with support offered, Shane was unable to complete his story for this book. I left the introduction to his chapter to show the real struggles we all can face. Even the other men, who did submit chapters, shared with me their difficulties in putting their stories on paper. As discussed in the introduction, this is a different shift in thinking to be able to openly discuss your feelings and experiences as a male. A new paradigm that shows strength in honoring your feelings and emotions.

I honor each person for where they are on their personal journeys. I thank Shane for offering to share his story, and I honor his struggle to complete the project. It led to sharing this truth that we all can learn from. Even individuals that have had awakening moments in their lives continue to work with limiting beliefs and old paradigms.

Speaking for myself, I try to witness my own limiting beliefs and old paradigms each day as I continue to remind myself of my own divine truth – a truth that is limitless and expansive.

***

Here is a quote from Shane:

I think I accepted this without a deep sense of commitment. I feel I've blocked any thoughts of the past, putting this off until later and later. I have an emotional resistance to believing that I even have a story worth sharing... Truth is that I haven't started, through no disrespect. I really truly appreciate the opportunity.

Thank you, Shane, for being the brilliant shining star that you are. You allowed for a new aspect to develop within the text of this book, for which I will be forever grateful. There are challenges most of us face, even in our own daily lives. Remember each day: you are beautiful, you are brilliant, you are amazing.

8

Wat Tam Wua Monastery, Thailand
Benji's Awakening Moment

In the summer of 2016, I felt a change coming from deep down within me. For the past few months, I'd had this sensation that I was being called to do something greater. However, to be honest with you, I was actually becoming frustrated at times because while I had the sensation and knowing that it was about to happen, I did not know the direction. I asked for clarity multiple times in meditation, but patience, trust, and timing were key.

Things were going well for me in Michigan at the time. I was working part-time contractually at a school district as an occupational therapist, primarily within the autism program. I had been there for several years, and I enjoyed working with the kids. I also co-owned a wellness center where I did CranioSacral Therapy, led laughter yoga classes, and hosted weekly sound meditation immersions. I was doing all the things I loved and manifested. However, something within me was telling me that there was yet another plan my Higher Self wanted me to do.

I was off from the school district for the summer, so I had the vision to go to southern California for a few weeks. Many times before, people had mentioned that I would love the San Diego area because of the warmer weather and environment. I do have to admit, I love the sun, ocean, and mountains. I had also gotten an email stating that there was a laughter yoga training opportunity in Laguna. Therefore, I thought to myself, *"All this is aligning for a purpose. Why not go for a few weeks and explore?"*

I started my trip with a week in Newport Beach while I took the laughter yoga class. It was wonderful to connect with and learn new material, as I had been leading laughter yoga classes for about a year now. I was amazed at the beauty of the Southern California coastline. I had been to California before, but not south of the Los Angeles area. After the class, I headed down to Encinitas, Pacific beach, and San Diego, spending a few days exploring in each beach town.

I felt a new passion arise within me that I had not felt in a while. When I arrived in Encinitas, it was later in the evening after my drive down the coast. I checked into my hotel and walked into town for dinner. I came across a gift store, and the worker who was outside said hi to me as I walked by. I said hi back, and we then got into an hour-long conversation about life. This immediately reminded me of when I lived in India. Could it be? I will never forget what he said: "Move out here. Come live your dreams. You can be whoever you want to be." This was true, and I have said it to others, but this time it resonated within my soul so deeply. Following our encounter, I went on to meet several others who would say very similar phrases to me. I thought to myself, *"Wow, everyone I meet around this area is so supportive and encouraging."* This was the community I wanted to be around. They were strangers, but yet they weren't. We all had the connection of being humans, and we all understood and supported that. To experience unconditional support and inspiration from people whom you just met was soul-touching. It was very similar to what I had experienced while living in India.

When I was in San Diego, I came across an event for a shamanic sound immersion and dance journey. I was immediately excited, as these were classes that we offered at our wellness center in Michigan. About an hour before the class on the day of the event, however, my back began to act up. A few years prior, I had three bulging discs and pulled muscles in my back several times. This was a familiar pain, and I experienced panicked thoughts of *"I hope this is not happening,"* and *"How long is it going to last this time?"* However, my higher spirit was telling me to stay for the event and do what I could without pushing myself, so I listened. I started out slowly, listening to the music and stretching out my back. Shortly after that, I was curled up in a ball crying to myself. I was going through an emotional release of allowing myself to move forward with ease. I allowed myself to feel the unconditional love and support around me and to know that it was within me. I cried for what felt like a long time and then got up and moved and danced with the flow. My back pain was still there, but it dissipated enough to allow me to engage in the journey even more. That evening was powerful beyond words. I feel grateful I was guided there that day.

Was this the change that I had been feeling for the last several months? It sure felt right. I felt that I was being guided to make the move to the Southern California area and allow this bigger vision to occur. It was already starting.

I was inspired by meeting all these beautiful souls, the gorgeous weather, and the environment where the ocean meets the mountains. I had felt before that something was missing, and I now began to think that this was it. Of course, the rational mind started saying things to me: *"But you have a business, a job, a house, etc."* Yes, I did have all those things, and that is exactly what they were – things. All of those things could be sold, let go of, and easily started again.

The decision was made. Now it was time to put it all into action. I flew back to Michigan with a new fire and passion. I was following my heart, inner wisdom, and dreams. First, I let my business partners know at our wellness center. Since we had very open communication, they already knew simply by me going to California that something like this might happen, so they were not surprised. They had also been there to support me over the past year while I had been feeling this movement, even though at the time I did not know what exactly it was or where it was going to take me. It fell into perfect alignment, as our lease was up October 1, 2016. Therefore, I planned to not renew my part of the lease, but I would stay until our contract was up.

Next, I called the school district where I had worked for several years. They were sad to see me go but encouraged me to follow my passion. Since the school year was about to start again, they asked if I could stay on for two months to transition the kids with whom I had worked. I gladly agreed, as I wanted it be as smooth as possible for the kids and everyone else. Leaving the kids turned out to be challenging, as I had watched them grow up and overcome so many challenges. However, I had to honor this new change within myself.

One of the biggest tasks was finding a real estate agent to list and sell my house. I sat in meditation, as I knew a few agents already. One in particular immediately came to my mind. His wife was a teacher at the school where I worked, and they had won a CranioSacral Therapy session I had donated for a raffle. Brian took the session and explored the work of CranioSacral Therapy. During the sessions, I got to know him, and what an amazing shining soul he was. I knew he was the perfect person to reach out to. Brian listed my house and within four days' time, I received an offer that I accepted. Wow, that was super quick! Reality set it in, as now I had an estimated closing date in October, just a month away.

What was I going to do with all this "stuff" in my four-bedroom house? Ship it to California? Drive it out in a U-Haul truck? Yes, these were all options. However, I was at a point in my life where I wanted things to be simple. As I looked around my house, I saw everything as simply "materials" – materials that I could live without or buy again if I needed them. What do we really need to live, to survive? Not much. However, some of the items were from my mom's and dad's house after they had passed away years ago. How could I get rid of these items? Again, I looked at them and saw that they were only material items. They were not my parents; my parents' souls live on forever and in my heart. The thought crossed my mind, *"If I were to die today, what significance would these items have to my family?"* They would do the same thing we did when my parents passed away – go through and take what they could use and donate the rest. I realized that we hold onto items under the impression that they are so dear to us and hold such a deep memory, and maybe they do at the time, but when we die it is our souls that live on, not the stuff we had. I was ready for a big purge.

I sent an email to my three sisters and told them that they had first dibs on anything in my house that they wanted before I reached out to friends and others. This had to happen soon, so within a week they came over and divided up what they each wanted. They took most of the larger items, which made it easier for me, as well as about sixty percent of my stuff. Next, I reached out to my friends, and they took about another thirty percent of my stuff. This only left me with about ten percent left. Out of that, I chose to keep about five percent, which included healing rock and crystals, Tibetan and quartz crystal bowls I did sound meditation with, and some clothes. I put the remaining five percent in a box and invited my clients to take anything they wanted. They took most of it, and then I donated the rest. The funniest story was my bedroom set. I had looked for several months for a bedroom set that I liked and had just found one in March of that same year. It had been less than six months since I had gotten my new bedroom set, and now I was moving across the country. I seriously considered every option, as it had taken me a long time to find the set I wanted. However, it turned out to be a great lesson for me. I had gotten what I wanted, and now it was time for me to let it go easily, so I did. A family member was going to take it, but then decided not to. Therefore, I posted a picture on my Facebook page that I was selling it. In less than fifteen minutes after I made the post, a friend who was at lunch with another friend saw the post, and she immediately took the bedroom set. She absolutely loved the set and wanted it for her new house she was building. I had to laugh, as I knew that when things are right, they flow easily. Well, this flowed very easily – within minutes, in fact. Ever since I had made the decision to move, everything had lined up effortlessly. Anytime I would feel overwhelmed by what was happening, I would remember how this was all being divinely orchestrated for my highest good.

When my house was cleared out, I handed over the keys and headed to my oldest sister's, Renee's, house. She took my mattress and put it in her spare bedroom, saying I could use it when I was in town. In addition, I had several friends and relatives all reach out to me and offer a place to stay at their place too. I felt blessed to have so many options during my time of transition. When the lease expired for our wellness center, I cleared out my stuff and said my farewells to all of my clients. I ended my last day at the school district and said goodbye to all my co-workers and the children.

Wait – suddenly, I had no house to take care of, no job to go to, and no business to run. What happened? What was this new sensation? This was the first time in my life that I felt complete freedom. While I purged all of my belongings and stuff that I had thought I needed, I felt a shift each time another piece of furniture left my house. It was like a death – a death of my old self. I felt as if I had died and my family was cleaning out my house, but I was actually still here to witness it. What an odd sense it was. I went through a bit of a grieving process, allowing myself to let go of all the things that I knew and held onto once before. I was in the process of creating a new me and a new story.

If I did not have any of these things to look after, take care of, or pay for, then I remember vividly thinking, *"I can do anything!"* Yes, I could do anything. Wow. This was something I had always known deep down, but now it took on a whole new meaning. If I could do anything, what did I want to do? The options were endless. Yes, I could go to California as I had thought, but I did not want to go and recreate the same thing I had in Michigan – get another place to live, another wellness center, and bills. This was a unique opportunity in my life, and I wanted to seize it. I was kind of overwhelmed by all the possibilities of what I could do. Where should I start?

In a meditation, I had a vision and remembrance that I had always wanted go to Thailand. This was it. I was going to go to Thailand to visit the monasteries and temples I had dreamt of. I also remembered that my friend, Nishant Patel, had been there last year, volunteering at an elephant sanctuary. He spoke so highly of that experience. *"Wow,"* I thought to myself, *"I'm going to go work with elephants, volunteer, and try CranioSacral Therapy with them."* I immediately looked up Elephant Nature Park and found that they offer weeklong volunteer opportunities. I emailed them, and they said that they had one opening left coming up in four weeks. Without hesitation, I took the spot. I was heading to Thailand.

I quickly looked into getting a visa for two months, as I knew I wanted to spend some time there exploring. Everyone around me was shocked, and so was I. I was supposed to be heading to California. I had already applied for and gotten my California state license for occupational therapy, and I had been looking for housing and applying for jobs (in fact, I had already received an offer from one). This trip to Thailand was a total curveball that I had not seen coming. However, that is how life works sometimes. Trusting and allowing the process to unfold is the part we are supposed to play. I had to trust deeply that this was where I was supposed to be next. I was beyond excited, and things were aligning to make it happen effortlessly. For example, my dear friend from grade school, Roni Vanderford, put me in touch with her friend, Sue. I had met Sue many times before – I had been able to introduce her to CranioSacral Therapy and she had invited us to her Buddhist temple for ceremony. Well, Sue had family in northern Thailand, and her sister had just moved back there from the States. Sue connected me with her family, and they graciously offered for me to stay with them in Chang Rai. I was amazed by all the beautiful blessings and alignments. I agreed and told them I would be arriving in two weeks.

I had a farewell dinner with friends and family. I packed my suitcase and was ready to go. The night before I left, my brother-in-law, Ron Ruffini, offered me his backpack to use if I wanted. On the morning of my flight, I got up and got ready to go. Right as I was about to walk out the door, I had a gut feeling that I needed to switch my stuff over to the backpack, rather than leaving it all in my suitcase. Even though it made me run a bit late, I listened to this gut feeling and repacked my belongings into the backpack. I had to leave a few items behind, as it had less room, and then off I went. I did not know it at the time, but this would end up being one of the best decisions I made. I thought I was going to Thailand for two months and then coming home, but to my surprise, I ended up traveling around the globe for eighteen months.

When I arrived in Chang Rai, Sue's sister, Lisa, picked me up from the airport. Their family home was stunning. It felt surreal to be in a family home in Thailand. The past few months had been such a whirlwind, and now – just like that – I was in Thailand. What started out as an innocent trip to California had led to so much more. Life is fascinating!

Lisa was a fantastic host. I feel so blessed and fortunate to have been able to start my journey in Thailand with her and her family. She took me around everywhere and showed me all the highlights, including the White Temple, Black Temple, and the border where Thailand, Laos, and Cambodia all meet. One of their dear friends and neighbors was getting married, so I even got to attend a traditional Thai wedding. What a special blessing that was. Spending my first week with them served as a beautiful transition into what was about to unfold. It was so comforting and supportive – an experience for which I will be forever grateful.

After a week's time, I boarded the bus for Chang Mai, as my time to volunteer at the elephant sanctuary was coming up in just two days. I maneuvered my way from the bus to the taxi stand so that I could get to my hotel within the old square of downtown Chang Mai. As soon as I arrived in Chang Mai, I fell in love with the area. It was bustling, so unique, and you could walk everywhere. I only had one full day to explore before my volunteer position, but I knew I would be back afterwards.

Being able to volunteer with rescued elephants for a week at Elephant Nature Park (ENP) was definitely one of the highlights of my trip to Thailand. It was life-changing in ways that I never even imagined when I had first signed up. I met the most amazing individuals from around the globe during my week there, most of whom I would see again throughout my travels or stay with in their home countries when I was there. I loved hearing all the different stories about how we had each been guided to be there that week. Each person's journey was so different and unique; however, we all had something in common – a love and passion for these beautiful creatures called elephants. It was truly heart-warming.

The owner of the park, Lek, has rescued over seventy-one elephants from abuse and tourism. She also spends a great deal of time educating the communities at large. I was surprised to learn that many elephants go through a tradition that is called "taking the soul." In this tradition, they are taken from their mothers when they are only a few months old, their trunks and all four legs are tied down, and they are beaten with a stick for four days, until they can submit and follow the commands of a mahout trainer. Even afterwards, the trainer often keeps a stick with a sharp, pointed end in his hand, and jabs the elephants if they do not follow the commands given to them. After four days of submission, the elephants "lose their souls" and are now able to be trained to follow commands, have people ride them in the jungle, or be a part of a show attraction such as being in a circus act, painting pictures with their trunks, etc. These are not normal actions for elephants, and they only get there through severe abuse. Therefore, by riding an elephant, you are supporting this kind of training. I am sharing this with you because it is important information that I did not know either. Education is the key to awareness.

Some of the elephants that we saw and got to work with had scars from the abuse or broken legs that were never healed properly, and some were even blind. Lek, the owner, fought hard to rescue as many elephants as she could (and continues to do so) so that they could live in peace and harmony. She said, "'Even if they only have one day or moment when they can be free before they die, it is worth every expense to rescue them. " The passion that resides within her still brings deep chills to my soul.

Some of the work we did for the week included unloading massive amounts of watermelons from the food truck, going into the fields and cutting down stacks of hay for the elephants to eat, shoveling piles of poop, washing the elephants in the river, and occasionally feeding them. I am not going to lie; this was tough work. Each day I was physically exhausted and tired. However, it was so rewarding to see what was happening behind the scenes, to get a deeper appreciation for what goes into supporting these beautiful creatures, and to get to be a small part of that. While we were out in the fields with the elephants, I would do small bits of CranioSacral Therapy with them if an elephant was receptive and wanted it. Yes, there is a way to ask permission of that soul prior to doing the work. They had already been through enough abuse, and I wanted to be very respectful of them.

After that week, I went back to Chang Mai without a plan for what I was going to do next. I stayed in close contact with my friends I had met during the week. As we were walking around town the next day, we came across a temple that offered a three-day silent meditation. The next one would begin in two days, and they still had openings. My friend and I both signed up. It was phenomenal to be practicing silent meditation at a temple in Thailand. After our time there, I inquired about longer stays, as I was used to ten to twelve days. They gave me a referral list of temples in Thailand that offered that, and I was forever grateful.

Another one of our friends had just returned to Chang Mai from a city called Pai. This was about the fourth or fifth time I had heard of that town in the past two weeks that I had been in Thailand. When that happens, I know it is a sign for me to check it out. I looked into the temples hosting longer meditations and found one close to Pai. How perfectly things were aligning. I would go to Pai, and then to the Mountain Monastery Wat Tam Wua.

90

In Pai, on my first day in town, I ran into Daria – someone I just met at the three-day meditation. What another great example of the beauty and synchronicity of life! The next day, we signed up for a tour together to explore some hikes and waterfalls. It was amazing to see her again and to get to hang out more. Since we were both only there for a short time, we exchanged contacts and knew that we would see each other again. Later, life would coordinate so we would get to explore the Thai islands together.

After three days, I navigated my way through the local transportation to find out how to get to Wat Tam Wua. I took the shuttle to a fork in the road about an hour into the drive, and then walked about a mile to the temple monastery tucked away in the forest. The mile walk in with my backpack was quite an adventure in the heat of the day. However, as I walked in along the road and crossed the path that said Wat Tam Wua, my jaw dropped. This place was surreal. This monastery, literally tucked away in the mountains, was so beautiful to behold. I put my bag down and a lady guided me to join the meditation in session. For the next ten days, I followed the monks' schedule. We would awake around 5:00 AM, attend morning offerings of food, have breakfast, do a morning meditation, a walking meditation, chores, lunch, an afternoon meditation, another walking meditation, free time, an evening meditation, and go to bed. They separated the men and women for sleeping. The men slept in a building with about ten guys in a room with two shared baths. We were each given a small mat on the floor to sleep on and a blanket.

This retreat was kept in total silence, except for the teachings in the morning sessions and the light talking that was accepted at meals. Thanks to the little bit of talking we were allowed, I got to know some shining souls while I was there. One of those souls was Benji. He was as bright and cheerful as the day. Benji always beamed with an open smile and heart. All the events that had happened up to this point allowed me to meet Benji, and I will be forever grateful that our paths crossed and that I got to share this experience with him.

***

Here is Benji's awakening moment:

Bodhi Moments

I was fortunate enough to have been born into privilege and am aware of that fact, but I always say that I am privileged in two ways. In one way, I am privileged by my being conceived and born by two academics, professors of History of Art, who paved my way through early education and at all times encouraged my interests in writing – and who continue to do so. In the other way, while my parents were teaching at the University of Essex, I was looked after by Edith Giffard, my childminder born in Gamache, a working-class village in the North of France, from where she left and came to England at the age of eighteen without a word of any other language but French, in order to avoid a life of domesticity and factory work and, instead, look after children. I was one of her first.

I am privileged to have been half-raised by Edith, who was Didi to me, because she showed me the fortunate life into which I was born from another perspective which gave me appreciation. She showed me community and endless kindness, loving kindness, and then she showed me spirituality. When I was six, she started classes of the children she looked after as well as those on the north London estate where she lived. In these classes, she taught us basic-level yoga and meditation, which, almost two decades later, I have discovered she looked up on YouTube. These classes were called 'Plant a Seed' and, if they were the seed, then I feel that I am blooming, with the endless petals of the Sahasrara Chakra, into who I am meant to be.

Although now we are more than dear friends, I didn't see Didi for many years after I grew too old for her to look after me. And, in her absence, my spirituality faded during adolescence, caught up in all my micro-dramas and insecurities. That seed was forgotten, though not lost, and lay dormant until my first time travelling. Whenever people ask me, "Did you find yourself?" I reply, "Yes. But then I lost myself in customs."

I was travelling in Thailand with my dearest friend, Jamie Hayhurst, unlike me in almost every way apart from the moral codes by which we live. We were in the ancient capital of Thailand, Ayutthaya, just north of Bangkok, and Jamie was bedridden with an ear infection. I was left to wander the ruins of the ancient capital by myself. To my surprise, I found myself deeply affected by the ruins. I felt a strong impulse to leave. I was scared, overwhelmed almost, by reverence. There is a word, the meaning of which I partially attribute to my feelings that day: a "chronotope" – a place where one can feel the thickness of time; the layering of history over history. Perhaps what I was experiencing was a sensitivity to the past that had happened there, imbued into the crumbling brickwork of the monuments, temples, and Buddhas, now bygones. Despite my strange fear, I was drawn to stay and roam on.

Just before nightfall, I came upon the largest site of the ruins in the city, which contained its highest temple. In the Lonely Planet guide, I was warned about stray dogs in Ayutthaya – a pack prowled the walled-off site, gently growling. To avoid them, I started to ascend the steps of the temple, the feeling of fear surmounting with steps, from which I could see the black cloud oncoming with the night. They rumbled like the dogs. I grew all the more nervous, my imagination uncontrolled and then, at the highest level, I stepped into the temple. I started to sweat, literally dripping from my body and into my eyes. I can't remember what it looked like inside, nor what I did there, but I remember stepping out again and onto the outer landing to see a sky engulfed by heavy cloud, Ayutthaya darkened underneath it. I descended the steps again and made my way around the base of the temple, stalked by dogs.

I came upon a shrine with only a dozen steps, up which I had the urge to climb. On the plateau was the statue of a Buddha, which was broken off from the left shoulder to the right hip, the top half of it altogether gone, though his hands remained layered and calm in his lotus lap. Though I hadn't done so for many years, I felt it right to sit

93

before the broken Buddha, bow, and then meditate. As soon as my eyes were closed I heard a thunderclap, which broke the clouds. I was immediately drenched in the torrent.

I sat for a very long time, all the longer to drown out the roar of the storm, the horns of the city outside the ruin's walls, and my own fears. When it all drained away along with my sweat in the rain, I fell into a trance.

I saw myself ascending the steps of the temple that overlooked Ayutthaya. I saw myself enter, but the temple was not as it had been – it was instead a room of pure white light and, at the end, sat the Buddha, broken from the left shoulder to the right hip. As I had done in reality, so, too, I did here and sat before the statue to meditate, with its image vivid in mind.

I'm unsure how long it was I remained, but when I opened my eyes again, there was a flash of silent lightning, with all else blinded but for the broken Buddha, wreathed in whiteness, exactly as I had seen it in the vision. That was conclusive to me, I had rediscovered my spirituality and I felt entirely new. All fears gone. I bowed to the Buddha and as I walked out, I passed the dogs, who passed me, untroubled by my presence. Before I left, I remember looking up at the temple, lit in an orange floodlight through which the rain cascaded.

That was the beginning of my travels, and thereafter I started to see again the things too coincidental to be coincidence, the patterns in the signs of life that weave together to create its tapestry. The patterns in the tapestry told me that I had to stay at a Buddhist temple. Specifically, one located in the mountain forests of northern Thailand, called Wat Tam Wua – the Temple of the Cow Bells. The urge was overwhelming and there wasn't much time left before my fight back home, but I was in the far south, on a paradisiacal beach the name of which I won't mention here. Soon as I had my route, I bade the beach and my friends goodbye, leaving Jamie's side for the first time.

The journey was over one thousand six hundred kilometres, and to even get to Pai, the town before the temple, had to take a boat, two coaches, two night trains and a bike. The night before the bike, I'd met a lovely lad from Birmingham on the train, who happened to have with him a bottle of Sangsom rum. We stayed up 'til sunrise drinking his rum from a bamboo cup a guide had made for me and, in return, I shared the weed which Jamie had given me as parting gift, which we smoked out of the open doors, through which the night roared past.

Needless to say, we arrived in Chiang Mai hanging hard and under slept. I would have stayed another night to recover, but I was on a mission, and so rented a bike and rode on to Pai. I had only just left Chiang Mai and was riding along the super-motorway, my attention flickering like a candle flame. I remember my last thought, "What's that thing on my arm?' and then the pickup truck ahead of me braked. My reactions were poor; I tried to hit the footbrake, but not soon enough, so I pulled the handbrake, and flew over. At least I'm not the kind of fool who doesn't wear helmets, but about five years have passed since this incident and I still have a stigmata-like scar on my right foot from the crater that was torn in it. I may well wear helmets, but I did not think to wear anything other than flip-flops. Other than that, I had a chunk of flesh missing from my right knee (shorts) and scrapes along my triceps and serratus muscles (vest).

Rarely have I felt like such a fool as I did lying on my back by the roadside, the wheel of my bike still spinning as though nothing had happened. Thais started pulling up beside me, helping me up, insisting that they should take me to a hospital. I thanked them, but worked myself back onto the bike, testing first that it, at least, was functional, and riding on, saying, "I need to get to Wat Tam Wua." The adrenaline numbed the pain well enough at first, but back on my bike, the wind whipped my wounds. The first place I came upon was one of the myriad 7/11s, at which I parked and limped in, dripping blood on the faux-marble tiles. The muzak they played in there sounded like a sarcastic joke to me, as I perused the aisles, collecting provisions. Making eye-contact with no one, I bought my provisions and left.

Outside the twilight strangeness of 7/11, I dressed the wounds. By way of experience, I had learnt not to trust the water in Thailand, so I washed them with the Thai equivalent of Evian, wrapped them up and rode on. I was relieved to turn off the super-motorway, but then there came Route 1095, the road to Pai, well known for its seven-hundred-and-sixty-two turns and curves, weaving through the forests and the hills. I had taken this road before with Jamie, but then I was confident, then I had not had a crash. I took the road slow and easy for the most part, until gathering rainclouds started to pursue. I was far more afraid of slippery roads than I was of speed. I remember, as I took a left turn, into the edge of the storm, I'd feel raindrops patter on my left shoulder, so as soon as I could take a right, I'd fly down the road and a little further ahead from the storm.

That was the way it went until I arrived in Pai, at a permaculture farm Jamie and I had worked and stayed on not long after Ayutthaya. As soon as I arrived, the skies split and I rested with the sound of rain all around and above my open-walled hut called Japan House, hanging from a hammock and surrounded in mosquito netting. Rested, but not well-slept, for the pain in my leg was a repetitive throbbing between the foot and the knee. That, and the mosquitoes had found their way in, the promise of my blood an absolute. I was too tired to fight them off, but that didn't stop them whining in my ear.

But I must have slept somewhat, because I woke up at the moment the sun crested the hills to the east. I lay there for a while, watching it rising until it hurt my eyes too much to do so. So I rose with it and drove into the town to drop off my bike at the rental chain. They were clearly not unfamiliar with their white, western clientele limping in all bandaged to return a bike. I had taken them up on their insurance offer, so they laughed it off, muttering 'Farang' to one another, a term which comes from the English word, 'foreigner'. Looking at myself, I had to accept that. And, in any case, I was now so close to Wat Tam Wua.

The minibus journey to the temple was a surprising agony, for every bump in the road shocked my injuries. Nor was I taken all the way to the temples, but was dropped off at the end of the path leading to the temple. I didn't argue with the driver, but then I didn't know that the path was three kilometres long. The path wound between forested mountains with sheer drops, along which I went, interchanging between a limp and a hop, given gentle encouragement by the Dharma flags that lined the way, flapping towards the temple. I arrived at lunch-time, for the monks, who sat eating beneath the statues of the Buddha, rose and flocked down the steps of the hall to help me up. They led me to a woman named Stephanie, who welcomed me and had me sign in. Lovely as she was, she was the bearer of bad news: my visa had expired the day before yesterday. Jamie and I had intended to go to Cambodia or Laos, but instead decided to stay and soak up Thai culture, forgetting that the purpose of the trip was for a visa run.

I had the option either to stay and pay a daily fine, or to hitchhike to the next town, Mae Hong Son, to the immigration office and extend said visa. At least I had the option, of which I chose the latter, whereas Jamie was where I had left him: on a paradise beach without electricity for most of the day and only one computer that could occasionally connect to the internet, which he would not be checking. In other words, uncontactable.

My first ride was given by a truck driver, who took me down the path that I had limped up half an hour before. The second lift I can't quite recall, probably because the third was so fortunate that it eclipses the memory. I happened to be picked up by the head of the immigration office of Mae Hong Son, who was driving back to work after lunch – especially fortunate as the office was located atop a very high and inconvenient hill.

Papers sorted and fees paid, I was driven back to the bottom where I waited at the roadside for nearly two hours for a pick-up. Shocked by how little sympathy my bandaged leg managed to stir, I eventually clambered into the back of a pickup truck where I smoked my last cigarette for the next ten days, enjoying every drag while watching the road snake away around the bends and curves.

The friendly couple driving pulled up at the end of the three kilometre path to Wat Tam Wua. They spoke zero English, I little Thai, and no amount of sign language was sufficient enough to ask them to take me the rest of the way. I gave up, and thanked them and limped and hopped up the path once more. The sun was setting, the

97

crickets loud, and the flags flaccid in the windlessness. My foot was swollen over twice its size, but I was too tired to be anxious.

I arrived in time for evening chanting and meditation. I was offered a chair, but refused, pertaining instead towards Stoicism. To kneel for prayer was agony. To cross my legs was agony, torn skin stretching over the kneecap. But I did, because for some reason I felt as if I deserved it. We opened the booklets, and the first hymn we chanted was 'The Prayer of Dedication and Determination'. Reading that, I knew I had come to the right place, rather than going to a hospital.

My time at the temple was remarkable, but it was not an easy time. Vipassana meditation itself is a mentally challenging practice, especially with a mind like mine, always away in what my year three teacher Miss Kermani called "Planet Benji." But as well as Planet Benji, I had to focus my mind through the physical agonies I felt, as well as the flies that swarmed me during the meditation, as they do a decomposing carcass. On top of that, I was deprived of sleep, having to lie on a hard floor with a thin mat that antagonized the injuries, throbbing on throughout the night without cease. Every evening before bed I had to slowly peel away the gauze from the wounds, which was torture, and only re-damaged what had healed.

Fortunately, however, they never became infected, for everyone there offered me their medicines and advice, and one evening before bed, a Malaysian woman told me to meet her at the lotus pons before dawn. There I sat on the bench, watching the sun rise between two mountains until she arrived. She told me to close my eyes and meditate on thoughts of kindness. Eyes closed, I could feel her hands hovering over my wounds, feel her healing energy permeating them with warmth. My thoughts were of all those present at Wat Tam Wua. I had never before, nor since, experienced such collective loving kindness. There was always a shoulder to lean on, always a friend to help me get my lunch and breakfast. I hope they are reading this, for they know who they are. One of the monks made a bamboo staff for me to carry; another, the ajahn, practiced a similar kind of reiki healing to the Malay woman; then one day, the oldest monk – deaf, mute, and covered in tattoos – saw my leg, and pointed at it in silent alarm. He scurried into the forest and emerged a little while later, holding a pack of leaves. He showed me that the way to use them was to grind them with a mortar and pestle, then to layer a leaf over that and bandage it up. The leaf proved to be miraculous. It not only healed and disinfected the wound, but the ritual torture of tearing away the gauze was absolved. Sadly, since the old monk was (and is) deaf and mute, I could not ask him the name of the healing leaf.

On my penultimate day, I remember sitting on the temple steps with Luangta, the temple abbot, reading him the letter of thanks I had written to the people of Wat Tam Wua. He said nothing but withdrew a bracelet of wooden beads from his robes and placed them in my palm. I don't think he ever knew my name, but instead he called me Superman.

On my last day, suffering through great pains, the ajahn's teaching came to sense: I was able to separate my body from my mind and observe my body, the pain that was it, as an impartial observer; to feel, but not to suffer from it.

Before I left, Stephanie told me that my presence at the temple had inspired so many who stayed there, in their practice and determination of meditation as well as that of loving kindness. I saw it as karmic balance: they did good to me, so good came to them. I left the temple with everyone there waving me away as I rode the way I came – by bus, bike, and train – back to Bangkok, from where I would soon return to London.

Since that time, the seed that Didi planted has further grown. Not only has meditation become a regular fixture in my life, but so, too, has yoga. I have been to Mysore, India three times now to train with Master BNS Iyengar, and now teach In London, or wherever I am needed.

Furthermore, after finishing my degree, I returned to Thailand and Wat Tam Wua with both legs entirely intact, where I met Rob, who asked me to write this.

I could end there, but I'd rather end with one last story within this story.

Back in Bangkok, I sat in a small alleyway at a plastic table, eating chicken noodle soup with extra chicken after the vegan hiatus at the temple. I was waiting for Joe London, a friend who would soon become my yoga teacher and introduce me to Mysore and BNS Iyengar, though that is another story. There I sat, when everything crystallized. My mind cleared and expanded beyond the skull into utter awareness of the world around me. Everything saturated, the changes in colour a shadow cast, and then the sounds. I could hear the cart of mangosteen being pulled behind me and knew they were mangosteen by the way they bumped against one another; I heard the conversations being had around me and through the windows above me and could intuit the subject by the intonations, though I knew little Thai; I could smell the subtle spices in the broth of the noodle soup that had been stewing for days; and saw the movement of the flies' wings as they searched around my injured leg.

Everything was intensified in that endless moment that stretched on, for how little or how long, I do not know. But I like that the most clarified moment of my life was had at a tiny alleyway restaurant in Bangkok.

9

Mantaray Island Resort, Fiji
Atu's Awakening Moment

In December of 2016, I left Wat Tam Wua, the mountain monastery. I was filled with a new sense of joy, inner peace, and stillness. This was good, as I was on my way to Bangkok. I stayed in Bangkok for five days, exploring the major metropolis city and visiting friends whom I met. By my second day in the city, I had multiple people stop and ask me for directions, and I graciously helped them out as best I could. A friend said to me, "It must be your overall sense of peace and openness that makes people feel guided to approach you and ask you for help." My feeling is that we are all on this journey together, so if we can assist each other, the better we all are.

Being in Bangkok for five days gave me a chance to regroup, check emails, reconnect with people, and determine my next plan of action. I was beginning to notice that this journey was becoming very fluid, with great emphasis placed on simply being in the moment. Often, this involved last-minute plans and changes. I knew one of my friends whom I just met at the Elephant Nature Park was down in the islands of Koh Tao, a place I wanted to visit, so I decided to go there next. However, the day before I left, he sent me a message telling me how bad the weather was down there – massive storms and flooding. Since I was focused on being flexible and adaptable, I changed my plans to meet my other friend Daria, whom I met at the three-day mediation and again in Pai. She was down in Koh Chang. She already had a plan to see four of the islands over the next week, and graciously invited me to join in with her.

In less than two days, I was on the island of Koh Chang with Daria. We were only there two nights before moving to Koh Wai. What an adventure this transition would prove to be. We had arranged for a slow boat to take us there. However, the waters were a bit rough that day, so they could not drop us off on the side of the island where our resort was. Instead, they stopped quite a distance from the island, and a guy with a row boat came out to get us. We slowly maneuvered our way from the slow boat to the row boat, amidst the rocking waves. They then handed our luggage overhead. Needless to say, some of those waves came overboard, and we – as well as our luggage – soon became very wet. I could only sit back and laugh at this adventure while the guy rowed us ashore with two wooden oars. There was nothing in sight along the beach where we came ashore. We collected our luggage (I had my backpack and Daria had a rolling suitcase), and the man in the boat said, "Walk to the other side of the island, and your resort will be over there." What?! Was this for real? It felt like a scene from a movie. Thankfully, a guy who was staying at our resort happened to be on that same beach, reading a book and relaxing. He looked at the two of us and noticed the confused looks on our face. He graciously came over to show us were the path was. This path would lead us over the top of the island, and then we were to turn left and walk another twenty minutes to get to the resort.

Still amazed by the adventure, we started our journey towards the other side of the island. This was another moment when I was very thankful, I had moved my belongings to the backpack before I left. Daria had her rolling suitcase. Another gentleman walking with us had his hands free, so he took one side of the suitcase and Daria the other, and they carried it up and over the hill of the island. However, from there he was going a different way to get to the other resort. Therefore, Daria and I hid her suitcase behind some bushes with the understanding that once we checked in and knew where we were going, and once I was able to put down my own luggage, then we would come back and both carry her suitcase to the resort. We were glad we did this, as it was yet another twenty-minute hike up, down, and around the cliff side.

When we made the last turn and saw our resort and the ocean, I was in heaven. The resort was very basic and rustic according to most standards, but it had such a charm, and the ocean was the most pristine aqua blue. I felt like I never wanted to leave. The lady at the reception desk gave us our separate keys, as we each had our own bungalow. The bungalows, again, were very basic and rustic – they only had a bed, a mosquito net (the windows were not screened), and a small front porch. This resort had shared bathrooms and showers. However, each bungalow was on the ocean front, so you could hear the glorious sound of the waves crashing all night. As much as we wanted to dive right into the ocean, we knew we had to go get Daria's luggage. Therefore, we made the twenty-minute hike back to her suitcase, both grabbed an end, and slowly made our way back down the ocean cliff path once again.

The next three days, I felt as if I were in a remote paradise. There were no cars, no streets, no bikes, and the only electricity was provided by a generator that ran for just a few hours each night, from 6:00-10:00 PM. You had to walk everywhere, and you could get to the other side of the island within a half-hour. There were two resorts and each had a restaurant, so you had two dining options to pick from. Considering that we were on a remote island, both restaurants were outstanding. During the day, tours would come to snorkel at the beach between 11:00 AM and 2:00 PM. Outside of that, we had it all to ourselves. It offered some of the best snorkeling around, with beautiful fish and a coral reef. Some of the other guests that I got to know said that they come back every year and stayed for a few months. I could see why. At night, they lit up the pathway to all the fifteen or twenty huts, and it looked absolutely magical. I met some amazing souls here. This island was not for everyone, but it was definitely speaking to my soul.

After three days, however, it was time to move on. I seriously thought about canceling the rest of my trip and just staying here, but deep down I knew that I could come back. The morning of our departure, we were blessed with smoother ocean conditions so the boat could make it to the front of our resort; we did not have to have the same crazy adventure as when we had arrived.

Our next stop was Koh Mak, where Daria had a friend who owned a resort. This is where I learned to drive a scooter/motor bike. I remember being so nervous when I was first given the keys, as I had seen so many travelers in Pai have major accidents from trying to learn how to drive a scooter in Thailand. However, this island was very calm with little traffic, so it was ideal place to learn. I started out just going up and down the street several times, until I felt ready to adventure off a bit more. Then I went off through the town. I had to check out several places and find a place to stay, since the place that Daria had booked earlier was full. This offered me good motivation to learn how to drive.

Over the next few days, I became more confident with driving and eventually explored the island with Daria sitting on the back. Having the freedom of the bike turned out to be really fun. I was beginning to see how each place I visited in Thailand had its own charm, lesson, and adventure for me. I was growing each day and exploring new boundaries within myself.

The last island we visited together was Koh Kood. I rented another scooter here, as this was yet a bigger island and we needed a way to get around. We also rented kayaks and paddled along the mangroves, which were stunning.

When Daria left Koh Kood, I stayed one more night to explore the island and get a new game plan. It was Christmas Day. I had plans to meet my friend John Moreschi (from chapter 2) on New Year's Day in Siem Reap, Cambodia, so I had about a week to myself. Therefore, I decided the next day to catch a boat and go back to Koh Wai, my favorite paradise, for three more days. I enjoyed every minute of it again. It was just as magical as the first time. After those three days, I headed back to Bangkok to visit my other friend before I needed to leave for Cambodia. My two-month visa was up.

Yes, I took full advantage of my two-month visa in Thailand, all the way through to the last day before it expired. Originally, when I left the States, I thought I was going to go to Thailand for two months, and then I would come back to the States to move to California. However, two weeks before the expiration of my visa, John reached out to me and asked where I was. I told him, and he said he was considering going to Siem Reap, Cambodia. This was a place I had always wanted to visit as well. Therefore, we decided that since my visa was ending at the end of December, we would meet there on New Year's Day. I was learning a new way of being in the present moment and trusting myself and the greater plan that was unfolding before me. Therefore, I decided during our conversation that I would continue on and see where this journey would take me.

I left for Cambodia on New Year's Eve. I had booked a hotel for the weeklong stay with John, but that reservation started on New Year's Day and they did not have an opening for New Year's Eve. Therefore, the night before I left, I searched endlessly for a hotel. Most were booked due to the holiday, but I finally found one. I arrived in Cambodia, went through customs, found a taxi, and showed him the name of my hotel. He took me into town and drove around a bit, appearing confused. He mentioned that this is the area my hotel should be in, but he could not find it. He stopped and asked several people, with no luck. Finally, he went inside another hotel to ask them, and they told him that the hotel we were looking for had shut down years ago. What?! How could this be true? How did Kayak let me book a hotel on their site if it did not exist? The hotel manager said that this had happened to another couple, and he was letting them stay on the couches in his lobby. He said he would let me, but they were already full beyond capacity. I was astonished. I was in a new city, it was almost 9:00 PM, I was tired from traveling, and now I had no place to stay. I asked the driver to take me to the hotel that I had booked for a week starting the next day. I went to the reception and told them what was happening. They were surprised, too. They said that they were completely full that night but would assist me in finding a place for the night. They must have called at least ten different places, but all were full since it was New Year's Eve. Finally, they found one that had an opening. They proceeded to tell me that they would not normally send me to this place, and that I could come back as early as 7:00 AM and drop my bags off back here if I didn't want to stay there. I thought to myself, *"How bad can this place be?"* I was about to find out. I did not have any other options at this point.

The man at the reception desk arranged for a new taxi to take me there. It was only a five-minute drive. Even the taxi driver asked me if I really wanted to go to this hotel. Now I really began to wonder about this place – if the taxi driver said this, then it must be bad. I walked in to the reception area, and there were bars on the window. However, the people appeared to be very friendly and welcoming. They gave me my key, and I walked to my room. When I got to my room, I saw a picture posted on my door with a list of rules for the place. It said:

1. *Do not use and traffic or produce illegal drugs.*

2. *Do not use weapon or smuggle illegal arm.*

3. *Do not traffic illegal sex.*

4. *Do not play gambling.*

5. *Prostitution is not allowed.*

6. *We hope and believe that ladies and gentlemen follow this regulation.*

7. *We are not accept responsibility for any loss of your life and property.*

My mouth dropped open as I read this, and then I began to laugh hysterically. What else could I do at this point? I entered my room and locked my door. I set my things down on the ground and did not even want to sit on the bed. At this point, it was almost 11:00 PM on New Year's Eve. I had been planning to go out and see the ball drop in the downtown area, but I was afraid to walk outside this guest house. Instead, I called my dear friend Candace and read to her the sign on my door, and we both laughed hysterically over the situation. I needed that. That night I slept on the tile floor next to the bed – or, more accurately, I tried to rest. I did not sleep much, as I heard my neighbors at all hours of the night. I think some of them were living there.

The next morning I got up at 6:00 AM, got ready, and headed back to my hotel at 7:00 AM to drop off my bags. He asked how my night was, and we both chuckled. We would eventually become good friends during my stay there. I then went to explore part of Cambodia. When John arrived later in the day, we embraced in a huge hug. It was so wonderful to see my spirit brother. We had met in Egypt, and now here we were, about to explore another wonder of the world together. It was also refreshing to see a familiar face after having been gone for over two months, and especially after the night I'd had. Over the next few days, we explored Siem Reap and the astonishing structures still standing. Walking through such history was mind-blowing.

Our original plan was to spend four or five days in Cambodia and then go to Vietnam. However, we came across multiple travelers that had just come from there, and they mentioned that the area was experiencing bad storms right now. Therefore, John decided to go to Thailand. After he left, I spent three more days in Cambodia exploring Siem Reap on my own and coming up with a new game plan. I knew that it was not time to head back to the States. I thought to myself, *"I'm already out traveling, so I'm going to keep going."* This was an opportune time to explore the world, to see and do what I had always wanted to do. This is what this journey was turning into. So many people talk about what they want to do or see, but rarely follow through with those desires. Their excuses and stories prevent them from doing so. *"Well,"* I thought to myself, *"I am going to do all the things I said I wanted to do. The time is now."* So, what were all those things I had talked about? One was to bungee jump off a bridge. When I had researched it years prior, I found that one of the top places to do so was New Zealand. Just as quickly as the thought popped into my head, I booked a flight to New Zealand that left the next day. Follow your inspiration without hesitation.

When I arrived in New Zealand, most people were shocked. How did I go from Southeast Asia to New Zealand? What a jump. Most people had thought I was coming back home after Thailand, and, of course, so had I. To my surprise as well as everyone else's, this journey was unfolding in new and exciting ways. It was about releasing all the old stories and patterns I had been running and allowing a new sense of freedom to form – one where I felt truly inspired by the moment and took those leaps of faith.

I sat in Auckland, New Zealand, in astonishment. Adjusting from the unstructured chaos of Asia to the structure of New Zealand took me a while. There were no dirt roads, people selling water and other items on the street, yelling out "Water, tuk tuk!" trying to get your attention, or garbage on the street. I had such mixed emotions. I missed the beauty and people of Southeast Asia, but I also longed for a bit of structure again – or at least, that's what I thought I was longing for at the time.

After a few days of adjustment, I tried to determine a new plan for how to explore this new country I was in. I could rent a car and figure out all the driving myself, take the public bus and figure out all the routes, or take a hop-on-hop-off bus that would drop me off at all the major cities along the way as well as offer attractions, such as bungee jumping. I just wanted something simple at this point, so I opted for the hop-on-hop-off Kiwi bus experience.

Over the next six weeks, I explored the North Island and South Island from top to bottom. I hopped on and hopped off the Kiwi bus, meeting new and exciting people each time, as we were all on our own time schedules. Most of the bus had a much younger crowd, but it did vary. I always seemed to meet the exact individuals that I need too; some have remained dear friends of mine to this day.

Another convenience the Kiwi bus offered was that we were guaranteed a night in the hostel in each major city where they dropped us off. This proved very helpful, as it was high season and some hotels were booked out. As the trip progressed, I began to book some of my own rooms as I learned tricks from a few other passengers at different hostels. I also began to learn what hostels were better, and which ones were places where you would not get much sleep. It was a learning experience for sure. Hostel life... it is not that glamorous, but it adds to the stories that you share later. For the most part, I was blessed with really good roommates. That was, up until the last few days of the trip, which I spent in a six-bed dorm room. The girl below me had sex with another girl on the first night, and with a guy on the second night. I'm all for exploring and having sex, but at least respect your roommates and go in the bathroom or down the hall! I chuckle about this experience even as I write this.

One of my major highlights from New Zealand was being able to fulfill my desire of bungee jumping the proper way. I actually did it three separate times – each time they offered it in a new city, I did it. The first time, I got to jump off of a bridge over water and actually partially submerse myself in it. The other times were over ravines between two mountain ranges. I got to jump into the open ravine from a small cable car that was suspended between the mountains. This was the highest and most exhilarating. I was so grateful to be able to experience something I had wanted to do for years. What a rush to fly so freely! I sat there in amazement; I had talked about doing this for a while, and now here I was, just doing it. I was fulfilling something so deep within my soul that even I was unaware of the levels of it at the time. The event provided me with the opportunity to deeply honor myself by following my own passions.

Another highlight of New Zealand was being able to experience the Hobbiton movie set. This is where they filmed the Lord of the Rings. It was amazing to witness each person in our group that day immediately become transformed into their natural child-like nature as soon as we stepped foot on the grounds. Each one of us were smiling and laughing as we skipped around from hobbit house to hobbit house. I had thought to myself, "*how magical that an environment can induce such a sense of wonder and playfulness in everyone regardless of age or any other label.*" For the past few years, I had a vision for a treehouse community wellness center in where people from all over the world could come visit, play, and stay. A place that would evoke this exact same feeling that I was witnessing at the moment. When you are in this state of being, your passions that you once had come back to life. For myself, this moment allowed for a bigger vision to occur. A bigger vision of a community healing center that offered a place to naturally evoke that sense of wonder and excitement within. A place that had tree houses, hobbit houses, swings, slides, bubble machines, and anything else that would bring about joy. When we are able to return back to a place of joy, the options and potentials are endless. I will be forever grateful for visiting Hobbiton on that day and sparking that vision that I hold so dear to my heart. I may not know when or where it will be, but this playful community center will come forth one day.

When I reached Queenstown in the South Island, I knew that there was only one more city to explore on the hop-on-hop-off pass. This meant it was that time again to start to ponder where I was going to go next. I literally had no idea. That was, until a friend whom I met earlier in my trip across New Zealand, Dustin Schmidt, sent me a message telling me he was going to Fiji in a week. I had never even thought of going to Fiji. I actually had to look on a map to see where it was exactly located. To my surprise, it was quite close to where we were in New Zealand. This sounded amazing. He sent me his itinerary, as he had booked a weeklong stay at three different islands as part of a "coconut package." It totally resonated with me to go hang out on an island with my friend and enjoy some warm weather. It was supposed to be summer in New Zealand this time of year, but the weather varied and was often cooler. Within a day's time, I booked my trip to match my friend's.

Five days later, I was on a plane to Fiji. Again, I had to smile and laugh at how this adventure was unfolding. Being in the space of simply allowing and trusting was so beautiful. The resort at our first island was right next to a local village. The people here were so amazing, warm, and welcoming. We immediately met two other beautiful souls, Sammi and Michelle, who had the same itinerary that we did. We all became good friends over the week. Soon, we would begin to experience what a "two coconut trip" was. The island and accommodations were much more basic and rustic.

After our week's stay of exploring the three islands, it was time for Dustin to head on his way. I am so grateful to have explored part of Fiji with him. This was our second country we had adventured in together, and eventually we would find out that there were more to come. I did not have a return ticket anywhere and had heard a few other travelers talk very highly of these two other resorts that were "three coconut," so I decided to check them out.

My first stop was Mantaray Island Resort. As soon as we pulled up to the island, I realized how different this would be compared to what I had just experienced. This was a true resort. It was stunning and gorgeous. There was a crew that met us with a native song on the beach. When I walked around and explored this island resort, I felt as if I were in a magical land. The dining house was set up on the hillside with sprawling ocean views. Every staff member had a smile on his/her face and was so beautiful to engage in conversation. *"Wow,"* I thought to myself, *"I want to stay here forever."*

Upon my arrival, I had noticed a big sign posted that they offered scuba diving lessons and certification. This was something I had wanted to do ever since that introductory dive in Australia. I wanted more formal training so that I could feel more comfortable with all the equipment. Therefore, I immediately inquired about the training. To my surprise, they had a class that started the next day. Wow, what timing and

111

alignment once again! Since I was in the right place at the right time, I signed up.

When I showed up for the first day of class the next day, I met our instructor, Atu. Atu had such an amazing energy around him. He was smiling, cheerful, and had a personality such that anyone would immediately like him. I knew he was the perfect person for me to learn from. As he talked, you could hear the deep passion he held for the ocean and underwater life. Over the next few days, I became more confident with using all the equipment, and my excitement grew each dive. Every time I was under the water, it felt like a whole other world, a whole new ecosystem. It was stunning and beautiful to see all the sea creatures, flora, and ocean floor. One of my favorite parts of diving is getting to witness the vastness of the ocean – seeing the drop-off in the reefs, and not being able to see where the bottom of the ocean even was, only complete darkness and abyss as far as the eye could see. That vastness inspires such a curiosity and wonder within me.

During our dives, I was able to see a large sea turtle swim past so closely that I could touch his shell, a group of manta rays swimming against the current, a white tip reef shark, and so many unique, colorful fish and marine life. The first time we saw the shark swim by, Atu signaled us to stop and be still. I have say, I was amazed, excited, and a bit nervous all at the same time. This was one of the moments that I realized that I was in an open ocean that was home to many other species. It was their home, and I was simply the guest.

I was having so much fun getting my scuba dive certification that I asked Atu if he had openings for me to stay and do my masters dive certification. My friend, whom I met in the first course, had to leave and could not continue on. However, it was divine timing as business was slow enough at the time that Atu was able to work with me one-on-one to do my master dive certification. I decided that because I was in such a beautiful setting, because they had an opening, and because I really connected with Atu and his style, that I would continue diving and get even more experience.

I have to admit, I had butterflies in my stomach before each dive. As much as I love the ocean and exploring, I was still a bit nervous since this was still something so new to me and there was so much to know about the equipment and various possibilities to watch for. We were going into very deep depths of the open ocean, and, as a CranioSacral Therapist, I know the effects a change in pressure has on the body. There were some days I did feel a bit off after the dive, as my equilibrium tried to recalibrate, and all the necessary gas exchanges occurred within my body. However, the joy and excitement of the dives easily surpassed any fears. I learned to acknowledge what was coming up for me, and then to shift my awareness into a knowing of complete trust and joy.

In my master dive certification, I had to do a night dive, a current dive, and a deep-water dive. The night dive felt as if I were in another universe. Again, I was a bit nervous going into the ocean at night with only a flashlight. However, I had deep faith and confidence in Atu. It was stunning to see what came alive at night. At one point we shut off our lights, and it was amazing to see all the things that were lit up and glowing. About halfway into the dive, we got into the current. This made me feel a bit uneasy at first, as you have no control. You have to float with the current. Always keeping one eye on where Atu was, I went with the flow – literally. To my surprise, it took us back to the beach in front of the resort. Wow, diving was teaching me more than I had ever imagined. It was allowing me to challenge myself in ways I could not do otherwise. I am grateful for each dive and each lesson that it showed me.

The next day, we went out on another current dive. This time was way more intense, and I had never experienced anything like this before. Atu ran through it with me, discussing what we would encounter and what to do. Again, I had deep faith in him and myself, knowing I would be safe and protected. There was a rope attached all the way down to a pinnacle at the bottom of the ocean. Once we dove down, we were to immediately grab ahold of this rope, as there would be a strong current. It proved to be so strong that when I was holding onto the rope, the rest of my body was literally horizontal, flying into the current. I thought to myself, *"If I let go of this rope right now, I will be totally swept away in the current."* Slowly, hand-over-hand, we worked our way down the rope to where we could see this amazing pinnacle. Then, I had to let go of the rope and let the current take me around to the other side of the pinnacle to where we would be out of the current and could explore. Trust. Yes, trust is a big thing within yourself. I let go and rode the current around the pinnacle. What a rush! We spent about thirty minutes exploring around and within this amazing structure, and then it was time to ascend. We had to work our way to the other side so we could catch the current, at which point it would send us in the direction of the rope. We were supposed to grab the rope as we went by, and that's just what we did. Hand-over-hand again, we slowly climbed our way back up to the top, legs flying behind us in the current. As we made our way back onto the boat, I was amazed and grateful for yet another beautiful dive – diving deep within the ocean and diving deep within myself.

Our last dive was a deep-ocean dive. You can only stay down for a short period on these dives, as there is less oxygen and you use more from your tank. On this deep-water dive, there was a ship we got to explore. It was stunning to go inside this large ship and all the rooms. While we were down there, we exchanged equipment as my oxygen was getting low and Atu was better at controlling his breathing since he was more experienced. After we did this, we did one more time around the ship before ascending. By the time we ascended, he was almost out of oxygen, so we did buddy-breathing. This meant that we were both on the same tank but using different regulators. As we climbed aboard our ship, I was stunned again at the beauty and lessons learned. Here I got to put to practice two of the important skills I learned in class. Atu said to me, "We did them in class and I knew you were good at them." I just had to chuckle.

I will be forever blessed by meeting Atu and getting to have him share his passion with me. Each time we dove, it was unique and special. You could feel and see the spark inside of him when he was in the ocean. The animals and sea creatures all responded so well to him as he would come near. Atu has a special gift. I know that is why I was guided to Fiji so unexpectedly – for these beautiful experiences and to meet Atu.

***

Here is Atu's awakening moment:

Bula vinaka, which means humble greetings to you all. My name is Atunaisa Kele. I am twenty-six years of age, hailing from a small Pacific island called Fiji. I am a scuba diving instructor who dives in the crystal blue South Pacific Ocean.

Today, I shall tell you a story of how meditating through breathing underwater changed my life for the better. But before that, let me take you on a journey back long before I started scuba diving.

This was a very sensitive point of my life, so please bear with me. I grew up with four siblings, three younger than me and one older. My parents have been divorced since I was sixteen. My dad was a drunk – an abusive husband and father.

Growing up, I was faced with verbal and physical violence. My dad despised my mom's family, and since I was named after my mom's dad, I was cursed at, beaten, and thrown out on our porch as many times as I can remember. Every weekend, my dad would have friends over and have house parties. The house would smell like beers and piss. And every Monday, we would have to clean up after them. As the second eldest, me and my older brother would have to clean, wash, and cook, helping our mom out or just doing it ourselves if our mom was kicked out that weekend. Every Sunday, I would look forward to attending the church service at my uncle's place just to avoid being at home. I looked forward to the weekdays, as it was the school days which meant I could just be myself and not have to worry about looking after my dad's needs. Life was hard, life was harsh. I could tell you more, but I will have to write a whole book for that. I hated my life; I prayed and asked God as to why my life was this. I had moments where I wanted to take my life, but I was too scared to. I was alone in this harsh environment, cornered to a point where I couldn't breathe.

When I was sixteen, my dad had an affair with another woman, who he is married to now and has three beautiful daughters with. But before my parents got divorced, my dad came back home, asking my mom to take him back. Heartbroken and confused, my mom didn't know what to do. You see, my mom loved my dad very much, even though he was the way he was. On that day by the kitchen door, my mom was in tears. I comforted her and asked her what she wanted to do, knowing that she was confused. But I knew she wanted my dad back. Maybe I was a bit selfish, but also thinking of what was best for us, I told my mom what I wanted her to do, which was to have a divorce and we, her children, would choose to live with her.

Being a young youth, I was faced with decisions that I needed guidance for, basically a father figure. Even though I had a lot of uncles who supported us, I mostly kept to myself and made hard choices on my own since I did a lot of them growing up. One of them was to leave the university and try scuba diving. On the semester break of my first year, my uncle, who was a dive instructor, gave me and my older brother a holiday job if we wanted it – to go work at the dive shop he worked in that offered young lads an opportunity to try scuba diving. But it was on the other side of Fiji. At first I said I wouldn't go; I was nineteen and at my prime. I was in my community's rugby club. I had all my friends here. I basically was loving life since my dad wasn't with us. On the morning after a big party with my best mate, who had a good job and was making money, I began to think of my life and where I was heading. I started to think about my family and the financial struggles we had. At least for the semester break I could make some money. And so I decided to take the offer and travelled to the west, which was a four-and-a-half-hour bus ride from home where I stayed with my uncle and his family. The day I started work with my uncle was the day I took a breath underwater, and the day that lead to changing my life.

At this point, my mind was broadened with ideas. I could make money for the family, travel the world, make something for myself. All this was wonderful because I had this opportunity that opened the door to this whole new perspective. But with all these, I still didn't know what to do and how to do it.

But thankfully breathing underwater, the calmness of it and not being able to speak, gave me more time to dwell on my thoughts. With nothing but the sound of my breathing and the view of the underwater world, it gave me more clarity as to what life was and what I wanted to do with it. I could compare the life of marine animals with mine, how it is all about surviving in a world that is wild yet beautiful. How all living things are born, learn to adapt, and survive. The more I breathed, the more I meditated. I meditated on my struggles and my opportunities, my weaknesses and my strengths, my family and my friends. This peaceful remedy, as I would call it, was what saved my life. It's been more than eight years now since I have been diving. I now earn good money. I am good at what I do. But most of all, I love what I do and love how far I have come.

I still face the struggles of life, like everyone, which is why I am thankful I get the chance to meditate on this through scuba diving – to be able to breathe peacefully and be in a good place where your mind just dwells in imagination. So, don't let the struggles of life put you down; there is always a way it can pick you up. Just breathe and live.

10

Kathmandu, Nepal
Garrick's Awakening Moment

After my adventures in Fiji, I traveled to Bali. I booked my flight about three days prior to my departure. The week leading up to that, I had learned that two of my friends, Anthony and Mary, were there hosting a retreat in Bali and then staying a few weeks after. Therefore, I decided to meet them after their retreat and check out another country that I had always wanted to visit. They had been there several times and really enjoyed the country. This time, everything aligned perfectly for me to go with them and check it out for myself. I was in Bali for a month. During my stay, I was able to participate in a five-day meditation retreat, stay in a tree house resort, engage in a local street festival, see the beauty of the land, and explore the many temples, waterfalls, and rice fields.

To be honest, I had mixed emotions while I was in Bali. I was with friends and meeting beautiful people. However, something felt very energetically "off" within me. I even got sick for over two weeks while I was there. Prior to my journey, I had heard many people tell me, "You should go to Bali; I could see you living there." However, I did not resonate or harmonize with the energy of the land at that time. There are many beautiful sites and gifts there; however, my travels through the country left me in a state of vortex – a place of irritation and unease within myself. However, I am grateful for all my experiences, as each one allows me to see and purge deeper levels that no longer are serving me. With that in mind, I am thankful to Bali for allowing me to grow. Bali was only reflecting what was going on inside of me internally at that moment, and I take full accountability for my creation of this experience. After traveling for several months, I knew that some countries could really evoke deep emotions.

After my friends left Bali, my visa was almost up and I knew I wanted to move on. I sat down in meditation to get some clarity. Japan soon came into my vision, so I booked a flight that left the next day. When it is time to go, it is time to go. I was looking forward to a new, fresh perspective.

When I arrived in Japan, I was surprised to learn that it was cherry blossom season. I thought to myself, *"I could not have planned this any better, but I had no idea!"* I was amazed by the stunning beauty that the trees portrayed along the streets and parks. Every time I came across another cherry blossom tree, I sat and stared at it with a huge smile on my face. I know I must have taken over a thousand pictures of them. I felt as if I were a young child seeing something for the first time. I had thought that surely, after seeing ten or twenty cherry blossom trees, the amazement would wear off, but it did not. From the beginning of my trip all the way to the end, I remained in awe of the beauty of these magnificent trees. I loved watching the petals slowly blow off in the breeze. It was as if it were raining cherry blossom petals all around me. I still vividly remember how enchanting it was.

I started in Tokyo and worked my way toward Mt. Fuji. Unfortunately, I had poor weather and was unable to see the mountain directly, as the rain and clouds blocked its view for the three days I was there. However, I was able to stay in a traditional Japanese room, which was amazing. From there, I went to Kyoto. This ended up being one of my favorite towns of my journey. This town and all its smaller cities were so charming and inspiring. The streets were, again, lined with cherry blossoms, and at times I felt as if I were in a storybook. Each day, I arose in wonder and excitement. I could not wait to explore another aspect of this city. Everything was going so smoothly – that was, until one day, when I dropped my phone in the toilet. I hurried and grabbed it, dried it out the best I could, and put it in rice. However, it acted very strange – it would turn on and off randomly, Siri (the voice activation) would come on by itself, and some apps would lock up. I had plans to leave the next day, so I hurried to copy down where I was going and the name of my hotel at my destination out of my email, just before it decided to shut off completely.

The next stop, Nara, was equally charming. When I got to my lodging, I asked if they had an Apple store or somewhere I could fix my phone. To my surprise, they knew exactly where to send me. They sent me to "the phone doctor." Yes, I laughed too; I had never heard of a phone doctor, but at this point I was willing to try anything. I went to see him, and he told me he would have to keep it for at least two days to dry it out and examine it. Not having my phone in a new city felt weird, as I always used my phone to take pictures, find maps and directions around the city, book hotels and plane tickets, and check emails. However, it ended up providing a nice break and an opportunity to practice relying on my own sense of direction to get around – a sense that had strengthened while I was traveling the globe. Two days later, I went back and found my phone to be as good as new. He had even put in a new battery. I was immensely grateful and gave him a giant hug.

Within this town of Nara, they had a deer park where people could feed the deer. I sat in this park many days, just watching the beauty of the interaction between humans and animals. It made my heart smile. In my home state of Michigan, we have a deer hunting season, which they say is to help control the population. I am not a hunter and, personally, do not agree with it. Therefore, watching this town engage in cooperation and peace with nature brought tears to my eyes.

I was in this town for four days. While I was there, I found and initiated contact with a place where you could stay with monks in temples. This town was called Koyasan. They said it was high season and that most places were already full. However, after a few days they got back to me again and said that they had an opening at one of the temples. I was beyond excited for this new experience. It was astounding to stay in a temple with monks, follow their schedule, eat traditional style

Japanese food, and stay in a traditional room where I slept and ate on the floor. I felt so blessed, as I had been able to do this in other countries, as well, and it truly warms my heart to be part of the local tradition while I am there.

While I was in the mainland of Japan, my friend from elementary school, Jill Bowman, mentioned that I was welcome to come stay with her in Okinawa, where she was living. It had been years since we last saw each other but heading in her direction next felt so natural and right. She was patient with me, as I did not know how long I would be on the mainland before I came to Okinawa. However, I kept her up to date on my last-minute plans as best I could. When the time felt right, I reached out to her and booked a ticket. I loved how this journey around the globe was unfolding. I never knew where I was going next, but I was always guided to the right place.

As soon as I saw her and Poncho (her dog) standing outside the arrival gates, we embraced in a hug and began to laugh. It was like no time had passed. As we began to catch up, we realized how many parallels ran between our lives and how much we had in common. She was even open to and excited to try CranioSacral Therapy. The following day, she came home to tell me that she had told her coworkers of her session, and now they wanted to try it, too. I was beyond excited to share this passion with others. Therefore, we transformed her office into a treatment room, and I began to share the wonders of this deep inner bodywork with others. I felt so grateful for this opportunity. When you are open to new possibilities without holding onto expectations, life can be spectacular.

To my surprise, I ended up spending almost three weeks with Jill. I had imagined that I would stay maybe seven to ten days. However, I was in the moment, simply allowing life to unfold before my eyes. I knew my next stops would be India, Nepal, and Tibet, and the extra time at Jill's gave me a chance to solidify my plans. I have to admit, at this point, planning felt a bit tedious. Couldn't I just do this last-minute? Unfortunately, I

121

needed a few days to apply for a visa for India, and to my surprise I learned that there were many things to organize in order to be allowed entrance into Tibet. I had to book my flights for all three countries and email all the necessary documents ahead of time, as I learned that these countries required proof of your departing flights before you would be allowed to enter. I also learned that in order to go to Tibet, you have to have a specific type of visa called a "group visa." Therefore, I had to find a tour company that would sponsor my group visa. I emailed several companies, trying to coordinate dates and times. I finally found a company with an opening that lined up with my anticipated arrival in the beginning of June. I wanted to be in Tibet for my birthday on June 5th. This was a special place that I had wanted to visit for quite some time, so planning it felt surreal. This particular opening was one of the last ones this tour company had, and they needed confirmation quickly to allow for the four to six weeks it would take for them to process all the paperwork and get the visa and other documents ready. The tour would start promptly after all the documentation was in order.

While Jill was at work during the days, I coordinated my next four countries. I planned to go to China with a 72-hour transit visa. China has a lot of regulations, but you are allowed in for seventy-two hours if you fly into and out of one of the cities they have listed. I wanted to go to Beijing and see the Great Wall and Tiananmen Square, so I figured seventy-two hours would be ideal. Then I would fly to India for a month to visit my friends whom I met several years prior, go to Nepal for four days to pick up my visa for Tibet, and finally I would arrive in Tibet on June 4th, 2017, just before the tour would begin. I did not care for being locked into travel dates; up until this point, I had allowed myself the freedom to simply be within the flow of life. However, this this plan flowed easily as well, so I decided to follow it and just see what happened.

China was a whirlwind. I was only there 70 hours, as I had to leave before my 72-hour visa expired. However, I'm grateful to have been able to see and experience the history of the Great Wall and to walk the streets of Beijing. Walking along the Great Wall, I felt as if I were in a dream. I had seen it in pictures and books, but to be there was fulfilling.

China was very different from most of the other countries I had been to. Their military presence was very strong, with personnel visible every few blocks along the streets. Most apps on my phone were blocked or would not work. It was a strange feeling. I told the guide that took my small group around for the two days that next I was going to India, Nepal, and Tibet, and I shared with him about my time in India before. He turned to me and said, "The Dalai Lama is bad." I was shocked at first, as I had never experienced this reaction before. It turned out that he felt this way because he believed that the fact that the Dalai Lama had tried to break away from China was bad, and if that happened, then other parts of the country would try to break free as well. Then what would happen to China? However, as we got into a deeper discussion, I soon began to realize that this was only the story and program that he had been taught by his society. Our truth only encompasses that which we have been taught, if we do not look beyond. I shared with him my experiences, and who knows – maybe it sparked a different way to look at things for him. Regardless, it taught me to continue to be myself and have compassion for all others, whatever their beliefs are or what truths they may hold at that moment.

After I left China, I flew to Dharamsala, India, to reunite with my dear friends/family whom I had met several years prior when I was there volunteering. I got off the plane, got my bags, and looked up to see Vikas, my dear brother (from Chapter 4). It felt so good to see him again after all these years. We started up right where we left off. On our drive back to his home, he waved and said hi to everyone along the way. Yes, this was Vikas – with his vibrant energy, he knew most everyone in town. He began to tell me that one of their friends and neighbors was getting married, and during my whole weeklong stay they would have different festivities going on. Therefore, after we arrived home,

I said hi to the whole family, changed, and headed off with them to have dinner at the wedding festivities. Welcome back to India. I already loved how things unfold and roll, and I was excited to jump back into it.

I was able to spend almost three weeks with Vikas and his family. During my time there, not only did I get to experience the wedding festivities, but I also was able to attend a life celebration tradition of a family member that had passed prior. While at the celebration, I was able to meet Nisha (Vikas' wife) and Vijay's parents, who then invited us over to their family home. It was fun to see where they grew up and look at old pictures of them.

Vikas' family home has four additional bedrooms that they rent out as a guesthouse. This is where I got to meet a lot of people from all around India and the world the last time I was here. On this particular occasion, I met another beautiful soul brother, Chirag. He was there accompanying his mom, who was doing a natural healing treatment. Chirag and I became immediate friends. Over my time there, we shared many deep conversations and enlightening talks.

Here is one story that sums up the beauty of this magical town and India. Chirag and I decided that we would take the twenty-minute walk down the mountain to McLeod to get lunch, and then we would come back. It was almost 11:00 AM when we started out on our journey. As we left the home, we walked past Vikas' hotel he had just opened, and he invited us in for a cup of chai. We had a cup of chai, enjoyed good conversation, and continued on our way. After another ten minutes of walking down the path, we ran into yet another friend with whom we got into an hour-long conversation. We eventually said good-bye and kept walking, and finally we made it to the restaurant around 2:00 PM. We spent almost two hours in the restaurant, eating, talking, enjoying life, and meeting many new people that came in. After lunch, we went into a few stores, just checking things out. At each store, we got into anywhere from thirty- to sixty-minute conversations with the store owners or other guests in the store. Then we passed a dessert shop and stopped in for something sweet and ended up here for another two hours. Each time we stopped, we began to laugh hysterically at how the day was unfolding so naturally. There were times others stopped to look at us, as we were laughing quite hard and often throughout the day. We were high on life. This was all unfolding so naturally from simply trusting, allowing, and being. We were definitely enjoying life and allowing the day to unfold as it wanted. When it started getting darker, we decided to head back up the mountain. Once we were back up in Upper Bhagsu, we looked at each other and realized that we did not want to head back just yet, so we decided to get dinner. We continued walking farther into town. By this time, it was at least 8:00 PM, and we began laughing again at how we had started the morning only heading to Bhagsu for lunch, and now it was the end of the day. We kept meeting people and engaging in conversations about life throughout the day, as we were not in a rush and did not have an agenda or a plan. *"This is how life is meant to be lived,"* I thought to myself. When you do not have a plan or a place to rush off to, the magic of life can reveal itself to you. What a beautiful gift that day gave to me.

I also got to see my first Bollywood movie at the theaters with the family. It was the best!

I was having such a great time in India that I did not want to leave. Chirag even invited me to come see his family house when he and his mom left, which would be in about two weeks. This was a perfect example of why I generally do not want to have strict travel plans to follow, but this time I knew that I had to be in Nepal and Tibet in a week's time. I also wanted to go visit my dear brother Vijay (from Chapter 5), who was living in southern India. Therefore, I said my goodbyes and went to visit Vijay. As soon as I saw Vijay, I was beyond excited. We had kept in touch by messaging over the past several years but seeing him again in person was amazing. I was forever grateful to be able to spend the next four days with Vijay before having to be in Nepal. I find such comfort in being around my brother. We shared many laughs, beautiful conversations, and cherished memories that I will never forget. He also introduced me to all of his friends, which soon became my family.

Again, I felt like I did not want to leave. I wanted to stay with my family. I had to reassure myself deep down that I knew we would see each other again. We had such a deep connection that I knew this was not goodbye forever.

On my first day in Nepal, as I tried to navigate my way through the busy streets to find the place where I needed to pick up my Tibetan group visa, I came across a monk. He stopped me and asked me if I were a monk and if so, where was my robe? I had to chuckle. Was it because I had a shaved head? I shared with him that I felt as if I were a modern monk. He then chuckled. He told me that I was a monk in many lifetimes that he could see, and wished me well on my way. After getting lost several times, I finally got to the place I was looking for, only to be told that they did not have my visa ready. What?! I had come here three days early just to pick it up, as I would then have to be in Tibet. He told me he would rush-order it, and I would have it in two days. Wow, this was cutting it close. *"Trust,"* I thought to myself.

Since I only had a short time in Nepal, I figured the best way to see the main sights was to take a tour. At the office where I went for my visa, I overheard them planning a tour for another couple. Therefore, I inquired about what they offered. The guy told me he actually had a three-day tour that started that day, but that I could join the group tomorrow and do a two day-tour instead. He also said he would give me a discount, since he felt bad about what had happened with my visa. This felt perfect and easy, so I said yes.

The next morning, the van picked me up at my hotel and we then picked up two more people. It was going to be a small tour with just the three of us. One of the people on this tour was Garrick Stark. We soon became very good friends, as we discovered how much we had in common. The synchronicity of life would again reveal its beauty to me. Garrick was in Nepal because he was heading to Tibet next, too. I immediately wondered if and hoped that we were on the same tour. Unfortunately, his tour was starting the day before mine. However, we were both going to the same sites of Lhasa, the Mt. Everest base camp, and the holy Mt. Kailash, so maybe we would get to see each other there. During our short two days of touring around Kathmandu, Garrick and I shared many visions and life experiences that resembled each other. It was kind of surreal at one point, as talking to him was almost like looking at another version of myself. I had always understood that other people are a mirror reflection of yourself and what you are working on, and that you will see in them what is actually inside of you. Therefore, I felt that life was showing me a very clear mirror of my new level of vibration and the beauty I was attracting. I was shifting my awareness to attract more individuals that were in alignment with me.

Garrick mentioned something to me that day that deeply resonated. After sharing with him where my journey had taken me and where I was going, he stated, "You are going to all the earth chakra centers." I had never heard that term before, so I looked it up later. He was right; I was being guided to various places around the globe and, yes, it appeared that many of them were areas of powerful earth energy. I love the synchronicity of life.

I could now see what the bigger picture was. Life was aligning. I had to make the plan that required me to leave India to get to Nepal at this exact moment so that I could meet Garrick. Ever since meeting Garrick, I knew that we would stay in contact and come together on a future project, and here is the start of that project. I am grateful for meeting his shining soul that day in Nepal.

***

Here is Garrick's awakening moment:

JOURNEY TO EXPANSION
BY GARRICK STARK

On our journey, we all have a story to share…

As our ancestors knew, it's only by sharing our stories that we begin to appreciate that we all resonate with each other's humanity… we're all living one life, but each of us uniquely perceiving our own experience of it. It brings peace of mind to know that we're never truly alone, for we all have the same emotions: hopes and fears, suffering and joy, grief and love… it's this ebb and flow that defines the duality of life!

We must be mindful that we are not defined by the story we are told by others – our name, nationality, religion, etc. – but rather, these are the projections of society's expectations, beliefs, and values that we adopt when born and identify with throughout our lives. But this is not who we truly are! We must find out for ourselves; let go of preconceptions, be courageous, explore through endeavor, and, in the process of our journey, discover who we really are.

All growth is essentially an expansion of awareness, as every new experiential insight expands us beyond the limits of what we previously believed our existence to be. In effect, we become incrementally more enlightened, personal experience layered upon experience…

On our exceptional journeys, each of these realizations leads us to see the world around us with new eyes. With an awoken gratitude, we can see with wonder and awe the blessings we have in our lives, but only when we have the will to push ourselves outside of our comfort zone, broaden our field of vision, and venture beyond our boundaries. To release our preconceived ideas and open ourselves up to the possibilities of what there is to unfold – ones we knew nothing of before we started on the path of exploration and expansion.

Embrace the strange and exotic, the challenges and exhilaration, so as to integrate new experiences, feelings, and sensations that, in time, inevitably lead to more profound understanding.

This is why it's to our benefit to impart our stories with each other. For it's this communal knowledge based on our experiences that offers us deeper insights, so on our collective journey we can all learn from each other - greater than the sum of our individual lives.

And so now to my story, I share with you some insights from my own journey...

MY STORY

In my humble opinion, I've had a wonderful life, one that I'm eternally grateful for every single day I'm fortunate enough to draw breath. There have been so many glorious memories, and yet others of deep despair; my life's been a rollercoaster with thankfully more highs than lows... and for good measure, lots of magic in the mix to add some sparkle!

I originate from Edinburgh in Scotland, though in truth I regard myself as a citizen of the planet. I don't see the borders either physically or genetically.

I was born in Edinburgh (Scotland) with an artistic gift whereby from a very young age I could visualize and draw whatever I imagined in my mind's eye... and I had a vivid imagination! I used to enter national and international art competitions, determined to win fantastic prizes which, more often than not, I would then go on to win! Looking back, I wonder if I manifested these amazing experiences, for I remember never having any doubts... almost a feeling of inevitability every time I made a submission.

I loved being in that creative space for hours on end, losing myself in the process, being in the zone and making my thoughts a reality. When in that state of resonance, it truly was a deeply meditative practice, verging on spiritual when connecting to my Higher Self...

And this gift has remained a core tenet of my life, as I've navigated a successful career in various design disciplines over the years: studying Industrial Design in Edinburgh, moving to Notting Hill in London to complete my apprenticeship in Product Design before emigrating to Ireland and diversifying into Brand Implementation, Online Banking, Corporate Communications, New Business Development and Consultancy in Brand, Web and Mobile Applications, and, along the way, Chairman of a national body for the up-skilling of designers in Ireland.

Now I'm currently endeavoring to become entrepreneurial and, in the process of working for myself as a Brand Strategist, consulting on identity, design, running workshops, and coaching executives – feel free to contact me if I can be of service. And more excitingly I recently became involved as a co-founder in a business with a new model for social banking... watch this space!

Throughout my career to date, I have won numerous awards and accolades and, to all intents and purposes, on the surface it would appear I had everything I could ever have wished for. Ticking all the boxes: a fabulously supportive family in Scotland; two wonderful children in Ireland; a successful career in creativity; recognized for my achievements; traveled the world to see the wonders; and, more recently, finding true love in my life.

But as the years progressed, I still felt there was something missing...

As some people know (and others not), my life has been profoundly impacted by many magical experiences that have fundamentally shaped what I have done and where I am going!

The divine spark in my childhood was without doubt my Near-Death Experience (NDE) that remained unexplored for many years (a book in itself). But ultimately, it led to my awakening in recent years, initiated by taking Ayahuasca in ceremony with a Shaman in the Amazon jungle. Afterwards, as I started to process and integrate the plant medicine experience, I began to embrace what happened that momentous day of my NDE and why I returned from the eternal bliss

130

of Source. However, one of the lingering questions that I was left with was: "Who do I want to be when I die?"

My life's purpose from that day has been to that end – who do I envisage being at the moment I finally pass over to the other side? Who do I aspire to be? This, in turn, led me to contemplate what I would have to do to become that person I wished to be and, as a result, every action I have taken from that day forth was in an effort to self-realize that vision I had, to live life to the full with no regrets. To live my truth!

New experiences stretch and shape us into who we become... as a result, we can never go back to the person we were before; we have irrevocably changed for the better as we have gained insights, both good and bad, that enable us to learn and grow as a human being.

We cannot unknow what has become known to us; it alters us fundamentally. It changes us! Hence why every intention and action we take - or don't take - makes us who we are and eventually will become.

But none of these formative experiences would be possible if we didn't make decisions, for decisions are the ultimate power we all have... to decide to do or not do. We are each the sum total of our journey, a continuous narrative that brings us ever closer to who we have the potential to be.

I could expand on any one of the aspects of my life I mentioned previously and write a chapter on each, but I'll save that for another day and another book! Instead, I'd like to take this opportunity to focus on my travels, my decisions to journey to the sacred sites and wonders of the world. Particularly, the spiritual insights I've gained from these magnificent, transformative experiences is what I'd like to share...

OPPORTUNITY FOR GROWTH

When traveling the world and visiting mystical sites, I've found around every corner, through every doorway, lies something that might inspire, enlighten or change us. Constantly confronting the *unexpected is one of the most electrifying and spiritual aspects of journeying.*

Travel is important, though, because it removes us from our routines and comforts, hurling us into worlds that often feel utterly exhilarating and, at the same time, overwhelming and scary.

From my experience, whatever you do and wherever you go, just allow yourself to be in the moment and mindful of the world around you. Make a commitment to yourself for your own growth on your journey. Take the time to integrate your spiritual experiences and watch your life transform...

MYSTICAL EXPERIENCES

The world is filled with wonder and awe, if we open our eyes to see it and open our hearts to feel it!

Our Earth's sacred sites that I've visited – the Great Pyramid (Egypt), Mount Kailash (Tibet), Machu Picchu (Peru), Tikal (Guatemala), Chichen Itza (Mexico), Lake Titicaca (Peru), Petra (Jordan), Glastonbury (Stonehenge), Dome on the Rock (Jerusalem), Rosslyn Chapel (Scotland), and also Mount Shasta (California) and Uluru (Australia), which are on my "to do" list – have all been designed by seekers before us for the purpose of fostering divine consciousness and the experience of enlightenment. Most sacred sites are built on the Earth's Seven Chakra points and act as a mirror to reflect the limitations society and our own minds have placed upon our true expression.

The self-awareness gained on a spiritual pilgrimage is special and unique for each wayfarer and is perfect, a gift from the infinite within each of us. On a spiritual journey, we have the opportunity to encounter our authentic self with integrity, clarity of mind and true purpose.

In the end, the most important adventure of all is the path to self-realization and the discovery of our divine nature, which I'm glad to say I have found to be true. To be happy in life, we must be at peace within and at one with ourselves. It's this internal contentment and

132

learning to cultivate the truth of who we really are that's revealed to each of us on our spiritual odysseys. These sacred journeys support us by nurturing a mindset of unconditional love, unencumbered by the judgment others and illusions of our society.

The magic of these experiences involves the opportunity to enter a dream state of oneness and expansive love so we can envision how life can be when we are living from infinite consciousness.

10 SPIRITUAL PRACTICES

Having the ability to see reality from another point of view, from another level of consciousness, encourages us to make healthier life choices as it broadens our field of perception. The energy of each of the sacred sites I journeyed to over the years helped me grow and learn exponentially, and in the end, that's really what I believe pilgrimages to these mystical locations is all about: personal transformation and expansion of consciousness!

And having a few simple spiritual practices while journeying can make all the difference to the magnitude of these mystical experiences. On my travels, these mindful practices have helped me sink more deeply into where I am at any given time, allowing me to discover a profound sense of peace, joy, or appreciation in the moment. If anything, by finding ways to stillness on the road, insights and lessons inevitably come to light:

1. Sense the Magic: Explore and feel the mystery of the most mystical places on Earth, true wonders of the physical world. Connect deeply with the esoteric nature of the energies that reside at each of these locations and let them resonate within. These magical places have the power to shift us, if we are open to change and expansion!

2. Set Intentions: Everything begins with intention! Like a seed
   sown, the "why" of your trip will blossom into something you could never have imagined. Here are some ways to actualize your spiritual purpose:

133

a. Write out your intentions, i.e. your hopes and aspirations for the journey.

b. Carry power objects that act as reminders, i.e. totems, stones, crystals, etc.

c. Speak your wishes out loud; manifest your words to make it feel real.

d. Create a memorable mantra that motivates you.

3. Meditate: To journey is to embrace impermanence. Through mindfulness, you can learn to weather the storms of travel, remaining in the "now" and soaking up every precious moment when you arrive at your mystical destination. Here's the secret to meditation: just breathe and do it, anywhere, anytime! It will help you be more present, to be centered, and navigate the challenges ahead of your arrival.

4. Offerings: When you arrive at a sacred location, take something of yours that has some significance to you and bury it in the Earth. Ancient indigenous cultures in North and South America, as well as Africa, traditionally used the seeds of sacred plants for their offerings. It becomes both an offering to that land, and a way to energetically connect yourself to that place.

5. Meet Interesting People: Your positive traveling-mood works like a beacon to other social spirits whereby you make heartfelt connections with new friends that resonate with you. It's not uncommon to meet other travelers with whom you can have a great time or run into locals who might invite you over for dinner or share insights with you. Either way, you will find your tribe!

6. *Learn to Appreciate: Speaking from experience, the important thing is to be grateful for your journey. Stay in the moment! And whilst traveling is amazing, so, too, is coming home. Return rested with a new perspective and with a renewed appreciation for life. Practice gratitude and watch the world transform around you!*

7. *Energy from Inspiration: While being away, you have the chance to drop a lot of tasks that occupy you at home. This will give you new energy, which will provide you with a fresh start. Gain clarity, open your heart, and stimulate your creativity. Be inspired, find your magic!*

8. *Embrace New Experiences: When you journey, you'll have a lot more interesting encounters than in your normal day-to-day living! I've ended up in the most amazing places – sunset under the shadow of a shining Mount Kailash or venturing into the deep subterranean chamber under the Great Pyramid – and landed myself in the most fascinating situations by keeping an open mind. Free yourself from the mental limitations and preconceptions that prevent the expression of your true potential and purpose. Embrace change!*

9. *Broaden Your Horizons: By traveling, you'll experience things you would never experience at home. Especially in exotic countries where not only the sacred places are wondrous but also the customs, the people, the food, and the landscape are incredibly different from what you're used to. By sensing these experiences in person, you'll get more insights about life and how it really works. You'll become that little bit more enlightened, coming to know things that you didn't know before: that's expansion!*

10. Memories for a Lifetime: Our end-game is to look back on our lives at the end of our days and have a smile on our faces, a lifetime in review brimming with extraordinary and amazing things that we've had the privilege to experience and accomplish. Judging by the wonderful recollections I have from my mystical journeys, traveling to these mysterious sacred locations around the world will form a major part of my most valued memories, experiences that fundamentally transformed me into who I will ultimately become!

All of the above spiritual practices will, in their own way, help pilgrims engage more fully in the magic of their mystical sojourn to these sacred sites and temples to wisdom.

And always remember, you are the author of your own life experiences, so start today: go explore!

WHAT IS YOUR STORY GOING TO BE?

We all have a story, our life's work in progress. So make sure it's epic, filled with wonder and awe, a story to share with everyone… and then regale to your ancestors on the other side!

Transcend your fear and suffering, be the best version of yourself that you can be by living life to the full. Decide today to enrich your life with meaning, have new and wonderful and awe-inspiring experiences every day you draw breath. For life is happening now, so grab it with both hands and don't let go until you reach your final destination… and then, I can tell you, that's when the magic really begins!

Decide today who do you want to be when you die; only then will you know where you want to go and, with that first step, you can finally start your journey of a lifetime with that one clear intention: to be the best "YOU" you can be!

So, explore and embrace your journey! Have courage and find a way to follow your unique path, have no regrets, and live the life you want to live – one that is majestic, soaring, and full of adventure. This is your odyssey that you alone can choose, be true to yourself, for within you already know the truth.

Start creating your extraordinary story today, a legacy to share for the ages!

THANK YOU!

It is said that love is blind, but friendship is clairvoyant. Thank you, Rob, for being a part of my life, whether for a reason, a season, or a lifetime…

GARRICK STARK | Contact Details

Email: garstar@gmail.com

LinkedIn: linkedin.com/in/garrickstark

11

Stonehenge, England
Dmitriy's Awakening Moment

After the delay, I finally received my group visa for Tibet the day before I was scheduled to go there. I was a bit worried that it was not going to work out, but I recognized that fear within me and tried to transform it back into the trust that I so deeply knew. Garrick was a good mirror, reminding me of this. Sure enough, it all worked out as needed.

When I arrived in Lhasa, I had a few days there to acclimate to the altitude, and then we would go higher each day of the trip. Walking around Lhasa and seeing the main temple on the mountainside was surreal. After many years of dreaming and wanting to visit Tibet, here I was, standing on the streets. I was so grateful for that moment. I met my group and quickly discovered that we were going to bond closely over the next ten days. Within the group was a family of a mom, dad, daughter, aunt, uncle, and friend, all from India, but living in Australia. They were on this journey to see Mt. Kailash, a holy mountain. I had only just learned about its significance. They were able to share with me the stories and myths behind it all, which was fantastic. In addition to their group, there were also two solo travelers from other countries. We would all become close friends on this journey we were about to embark on.

My second day there was June 5, 2017. It was my forty-second birthday. I felt blessed to be able to spend my birthday in a place that I had always wanted to be. As the magic of life would show me, it turned out that there were three of us on this trip that all would celebrate birthdays. I loved this. During this day, we visited Potala Palace, the main temple in town that is in all the famous pictures and was once the Dalai Lama's winter home. I was vibrating with buzzing energy as we walked through the many chambers of the temple and listened to monks chanting in the distance. There was a feeling of familiarity, as if it were a place that I knew or had been before. This may have come from the many temples I had visited before in other countries, but also I have been shown through many different kinds of readings that I have lived lifetimes as a monk and spiritual guide. I knew this to be true, as I could not otherwise explain the feeling that I had when I visited places such as these.

That evening, we were blessed to be able to attend a local Tibetan dinner show. Our guide had arranged a birthday song and dessert for me, and he even came out and blessed me with a white adornment and gave me a small Buddhist monk figurine. This figurine would soon be the mascot of the trip. One of the other travelers, Bonnie, also had a small figurine (named Lara), which she was including in her pictures. Our two figurines quickly became friends and were in multiple pictures together throughout the adventure in Tibet. This added an element of fun and silliness to what we were about to explore and see, as Tibet holds very deep, strong, intense energy. The land itself and the history there have been through some very tragic times with the Chinese government, including mass killings and bombings of the Tibetan people. I had been aware of this prior to my trip, but being there provided a completely different sense as I stood in the middle of where it occurred. There were days I struggled with maintaining a sense of grounded peace due to this emotional charge.

Though I was beyond excited to see and be in Tibet, I did not realize the depths to which I would feel the energy of the tragedy from the past – though I suppose it was not a surprise, since I know I am very empathetic. I feel that is often why I am guided to these various regions; it provides an excellent opportunity for me to practice noticing what is happening by feeling it, but not getting pulled into it as well. Learning to remain compassionate and as neutral as possible is a beautiful life lesson, as we all see and face challenges each and every day. Here, I thought I was coming to Tibet to see the temples and have fun – which I did – but there was a much deeper and bigger picture that was occurring within me. My Higher Self guided me here for that exact reason.

Our guide shared with us how he had tried to escape Tibet and go to Nepal on two separate occasions by crossing through the treacherous Himalayan mountain ranges. However, he got caught by the Chinese government each time and was put in prison for his attempts. Following his second attempt, he met his wife and gave up trying to leave. Listening to his stories reminded me of the time I was volunteering in India, teaching the monks English. The monks had shared with me their individual stories of what occurred and what they had witnessed as they escaped via the route through the mountain ranges. It was heart-wrenching to see the attempts by these individuals and what they would sacrifice for a sense of freedom.

After we left Lhasa, we slowly made our way to the Mt. Everest base camp. Wow! Standing there at the base of Mt. Everest, the highest mountain in the world, was another surreal moment. As you stand there before it, you can feel the powerful energy this mountain range radiates. I could also definitely notice the change to the higher altitude, and the temperatures were much colder. However, we were still able to do a small trek to scope out this amazing beauty. I was enthralled by how some climbers attempt to make their way to the top of this giant, and also took into account how many souls were lost trying. Just a few weeks prior, a famous climber had died on his way back down.

That night when we went to bed at the base camp, I felt very strange and knew that something was not right. I was lightheaded and was starting to get the chills. Up until this point, I had experienced my body adjusting to the altitude each day with slight headaches and a sense of being "high," but I would adjust with time. Therefore, I went ahead to bed. I slept in all of my winter clothes, a jacket, a hat, and I had five woolen blankets on top of me. Each time I tried to roll onto my side during the night, I immediately became very short of breath and had to wait to regain my breathing. This scared me, as I knew something was wrong. At moments like these, I appreciate my ability to meditate and regain a sense of calmness to make it through the intensity. As early morning came, I began to hear others awaken. I quickly shared with my guide and friends what was occurring. My guide encouraged me to sit up. However, when I did, I felt very weak, dizzy, and as if I were going to pass out. He said that yes, it was likely altitude sickness, and he went to get the emergency oxygen. I laid there on my side while I tried my best to breathe in this oxygen treatment, even though all I wanted was to fall back and drift in unconsciousness. After twenty minutes of this treatment, I began to feel slightly better, but I was still very weak. My guide explained to me that we were at Mt. Everest base camp with nothing around, and it would take about eight to ten hours to get to the next major town where they had medical assistance. They assisted me in walking to the van, and I climbed in and laid down on the back bench.

The drive was very challenging for me. I stayed in a fetal position most of the trip. When they stopped for lunch, they encouraged me to try to come into the restaurant. However, I knew that I did not have the strength and that it was best for me to continue resting in the van. My friends on the trip provided me with snacks and crackers – something light to manage. When we pulled into town later that day, I had never been so happy to be somewhere. My fever had begun to spike multiple times on the trip, but I was taking aspirin to offset it. Our guide took me to the clinic in town, which consisted of a small exam room and four treatment beds. The doctor examined me immediately and knew right away that I was experiencing altitude sickness. He gave me two shots for the fever, hooked me up to an IV because I was severely dehydrated, and put me on oxygen. I laid there in the room for almost two hours, allowing my body to take in all that was depleted. There were two other individuals in there with me that were experiencing altitude sickness as well. The doctor mentioned that it was a very common thing in that area.

However, he also said that it was important that I came in for treatment when I did.

While I lay there in bed, our guide got a call from the head office of the tour company. He updated them on what was happening. They stated that they had another tour coming back from Mt. Kailash the next day and could pick me up and bring me back to Lhasa if I wanted or needed. I thought to myself, *"I came this far; I want to keep going."* The doctor reassured me that I would probably continue to feel better after the treatment. Our guide stayed with me the whole time that I was at the clinic, as he had to translate for me.

After receiving pure oxygen and electrolytes for over two hours, my body felt much more alive again. Wow – what a crazy twenty-four hours that was! At one point during the night before, I had visions of myself dying there at Mt. Everest. However, it was not my time yet, and, therefore, my soul found an inner strength to carry on. It is amazing to witness the deep power of the soul and willingness to live. That night, I went back to my room and slept for over ten hours, as my body needed it.

The next morning, I felt much better – not at my full capacity or strength, but definitely improving. That day we had a shorter drive of only six hours to make it to the next town. This was the day before we were to embark on our three-day trek/kora around Mt. Kailash. I thought to myself, *"I am not sure my body is ready to trek and climb a mountain after what it just went through."* However, I told myself I would play it by ear and see in the morning if I was ready and able to trek.

The morning came, and it was time to begin day one of our treks around Mt. Kailash. I thought to myself, *"Just over twenty-four hours ago I was lying in a clinic bed, hooked up to IVs and oxygen because I was so faint and weak, and here I am about to trek ten hours on my first day. Am I crazy?"* Maybe. However, there was something within myself that was pulling and guiding me forward. I decided I would just take my time and take breaks if needed, and so the journey began. For the most part, the beginning of the trek was fairly flat, which made it better for me at that time. As the day progressed, the trail became a bit more elevated, and we began hiking both up and down. By the time we reached camp for the night, I had trekked for over ten hours and my body was completely exhausted. The last two hours of the trek were a bit challenging as I felt the fatigue kick in. This is when I realized that my body was indeed still recovering.

That night during dinner, my body was very sore and fatigued. I began to feel lightheaded, chilled, and generally "not right" again. The fever was coming back. It was snowing and very cold, and I knew that day two of the kora was even more extreme, as we would be going higher in altitude and there would be no way to turn back. I had to take a look at my old patterns and stories, as in the past I would often push myself through difficult situations. Here I was again. I was grateful I made it to the base of Mt. Kailash so that I could engulf myself in the energy it emitted. However, did I really need to push my body just to finish a three-day kora? I did not even know what the kora was until a week ago. No, I was here to listen to and honor myself and my body's temple. My body and Higher Self wanted me to experience Mt. Kailash, and that was it. Therefore, I told my guide that I was unable to go on and finish the next two days. He completely understood my decision and told me that I could either walk back down on the same route we just came up, or they had transportation that would come up and get those that could not make it. At that point, my body was shutting down again and another ten-hour trek was not what I needed, so I opted for the ride down. Once I made that decision, four other people from my group decided to join me and not continue on either. This was the best decision for me to honor myself.

The next morning, my friend Bonnie and I got up and did a small, twenty-minute hike to the base of Mt. Kailash that was right there at our camp. As we both sat there, amazed by the stunning beauty of pure bliss that it radiated, we knew that this was why we did not move forward. The other three people in our group had to leave before 6:00 AM that day and were unable

143

to enjoy the full beauty of this mountain front. We were able to sit there for over two hours, enjoying, meditating, and witnessing the presence of this magnificent mountain range. I was filled with pure love and compassion that morning. My Higher Self wanted me to connect on a deeper level with the energy present, and I was able to do so by choosing not to complete a task that *others* had told me would assist with my enlightenment. This was another beautiful lesson given to me at that moment, reinforcing the importance of following and trusting my own inner guide and wisdom. That morning that I spent basking in the bliss of the mountain flow will be forever in my heart.

While we waited for the others in our group to complete the kora, we rested in a nice hotel room and recovered. As I rested for those two days, I realized I had underestimated how much my body really needed that time to rest. My physical body had gone through a lot, but I was also processing on many levels – emotionally and spiritually. At one point, I thought to myself, *"I am ready to be on sea/ground level again."* Even as we rested in the room, I was still experiencing headaches and the effects of altitude. I never even thought or imagined altitude when I was planning my Tibet trip. This came as an unexpected surprise. I had been trekking in Machu Picchu and many other mountain ranges before with ease.

When we reached Lhasa again, I was excited to be back in a warmer climate and lower elevation, even though we were still high. Our tour had come to an end, and I was thankful for all the life lessons I had encountered along the way. Thank you, Tibet, for the deep growth physically, emotionally, and spiritually.

Since I had been required to book an exit flight from Tibet before my arrival, I had arrangements in place to go back to Nepal. However, at that point, I was not feeling guided to stay there longer. I knew I wanted to visit Europe before heading back to Michigan in August for my nephew's wedding, so I booked a connecting flight from Nepal to Amsterdam. While in

Amsterdam, my friend Dustin, whom I had met in New Zealand and then traveled with to Fiji, decided to drive over and meet me since he was living in Germany at the time. Following our three-day adventure in Amsterdam, we drove to Dustin's house in Germany, and I got to experience the autobahn. He showed me around his hometown for another three days before I went to go meet my cousins in Paris. We had to laugh, as now this was the fourth country we were in together in a short six-month time period: New Zealand, Fiji, the Netherlands, and Germany. It is beautiful to witness how life unfolds so unexpectedly. I never knew or imagined I would get to reconnect with this amazing soul in so many places.

Speaking of the synchronicity of life, while I was in Paris, I met up with a person whom Dustin and I had met at a park in Amsterdam a few days prior. It was fun to see a familiar face, share a meal again, and explore a new city. Of course, since I was in Paris, I had to make the trip to the top of the Eiffel Tower. Looking out over the city and waterways was another magical moment; I felt so blessed to be able to experience my dreams coming true, visiting all these gorgeous places that I had always wanted to see.

My cousins soon began to arrive, and we headed to the south of France, as they had won a villa in a raffle auction. It was wonderful to see some familiar faces of family after being gone and traveling for almost a year. Being in southern France felt as if I were in a story book. The little villas and towns were beyond charming. One day we went hot air ballooning, which added even more magic to our time there as we drifted above castles and wine villages.

After France, I had originally planned on going to England. However, again at the last minute, I instead got inspiration and guidance to go to Portugal. Over the last week, I had come across several people that shared stories of how much they loved Portugal. This had not even been on my radar or consideration, but something told me to explore it. Once I looked into Portugal,

I soon remembered that this was a place I had wanted to visit several years prior. This was one of the places where they offered the opportunity to swim with dolphins in the wild ocean, their home. I love dolphins and whales, and to have the opportunity to swim with them would be magical since it was in the ocean where they are free to swim on their own. I once swam with them in an aquarium park, and ever since that day I have promised myself that I would never do that again. Dolphins should not be used in a park or aquarium as an attraction. They should be free to swim in the ocean, as that is their home. Swimming with dolphins in the open ocean is different, as they can swim away if they choose and not interact.

I was super excited. I had not realized how close I was to Portugal, and I had forgotten about being able to swim with dolphins in the Azores Islands. Since I had to catch a flight out of Lisbon, I decided to stay there for a few days to check out the town. Wow – I was impressed. This was a town I had not expected to come to, and it was gorgeous. The many pastel-colored buildings and houses I passed while walking through town were stunning. I was so happy I was guided in this direction at the last minute. There are many twists and turns to life, and the unexpected ones have a tendency to be the best ones. Either that, or they have the most important lesson to show us. I have come to learn that when I have expectations around something, that is often when I get disappointed. I am the one who puts limitations on what I am going to feel or experience. When my expectations are not met, I notice feelings of sadness or disappointment. This is all caused by me. When I do not have expectations and simply go with an open mind, following my own inner guidance, then I often feel more joy. This is because I am now experiencing things around which I had no limits or guidelines. I am able to fully immerse myself within the experience and see the wonder and joy it has to offer. What a difference it can make to our outlook.

When I got to the Azores, I was beyond excited. I was there for a week and ended up going out with the dolphins on four

146

separate occasions. I really respected the way they handled the tours. When we came across a pod of dolphins, we would hang out with them and see if they wanted to interact. If they did, then (and only then) they would allow two people to get in the water at a time to snorkel with them, with the understanding that we could not touch the dolphins or disturb them. We could snorkel along with them, but if they swam away, then we had to allow them that freedom. In addition, if there was already a boat in the area and it was a small pod, then we were not allowed in the water as it would be too much for the dolphins. I really honored how much they respected the dolphins, as this is how it should be. This was the dolphins' home, and we were guests in their environment.

My heart was so full from being able to swim and be in the water with these gentle and beautiful creatures. However, it was time to go to England. I was off to London, another town I had always wanted to experience. Yes, this journey was unfolding into just that. A journey of going to all the places I always wanted to see and experience. My Higher Self was the guide, and I was simply allowing it to unfold.

London was just as fascinating as I had imagined, with double-decker buses, bustling streets, and busy waterways. I did all the touristy stuff as I explored the area. However, as I was exploring, I came across an event that caught my eye. It was an event put on by the London College of Spirituality that consisted of a meditation, inner journey, and energy transmission. I thought to myself, *"This is right up my alley and interests."* I also saw that they had a group event going to crop circles one day and Stonehenge the next. Wow, this was perfect – two things of deep interest to me. I figured I would go to the meditation event first to check out the energy there, and then, if I liked it, I would commit to the other two days.

During the meditation, I felt very supported in the space and was able to go deep within. I knew that this was exactly where I needed to be. I was experiencing that deep knowing of life aligning again, bringing me to the right place at the right time.

The next day, I met this amazing group again as we headed out to the crop circles. I was smiling ear-to-ear; I felt so lucky to be able to experience this. I gave gratitude to my Higher Self for guiding me to this group. I had wanted to visit crop circles anyway, and this was the perfect group to do it with. They understood the magnitude of creation and the magic of life's work.

Each crop circle we visited that day had its own unique energy and vibration. This made sense to me, as each crop was formed into its own unique geometric shape. Each shape creates a different effect of how energy is created and carried. It varied so much. At one of the circles we visited, I wanted to leave as soon as we got there. I was able to witness how I was feeling and explore it, but I did not want to stay. However, at another one we visited, I could not wait to get out of the van and run right into the circle. It felt very playful and fun, as if I could stay there all day. The mystery of the crop circles was amazing to witness and be a part of.

That night, after getting back from the crop circles outside of London, I was buzzing with energy. I felt as if my cellular DNA was shifting and making adjustments. Eventually, I did manage to fall asleep. I awoke very early the next day to meet the group again, as were going to Stonehenge. This was a huge day for me!!! It was July 23, 2017. This was a place I had wanted to visit and experience for quite some time now. I have been guided to many sacred sites around the globe, and I was definitely looking forward to this one. I felt as if I were a little kid. I was so excited, and I could not wait to take the train to meet the group and get there.

On the van ride there, I got into conversation with the others about our evenings the night before, our crop circles experiences, and what had brought us to the point of heading to Stonehenge. You could feel the excitement build. There were a few new people on the van ride that day that had not been able to make it to the crop circles. One of those individuals was Dmitriy. He emanated such a vibrant energy about him. His eyes were wide open and ready to experience all that was available to life.

About five minutes before we pulled up to Stonehenge, my cells started to buzz again very intensely. When this happens, it feels as if every cell in my body is being activated – they become tingly and buzzy. When it gets extremely intense, as it did at that moment, I begin to laugh because the sensation feels so good. I become so full of joy that I beam out a smile as big as I can make it.

While we were waiting for them to get our tickets so we could to enter, I got into a good conversation with Dmitriy about energy and what I was feeling. He shared some similar experiences. We got our tickets and entered into the vortex of Stonehenge. We had about thirty minutes to wander around on our own before we would do a group ceremony. I went in the directions that I felt guided to go and sat in meditation. Wow – I felt as if I were going to blast out of there with all this energy surging through me. Then it came time for our ceremony. They played quartz crystal bowls and instruments for a sound immersion to assist us with a deeper connection. I was familiar with this, as this is what we had offered at our wellness center. Before the bowls began, I was already on a deep journey within. I felt a deep connection pull within the ground, and I could feel the universe showing me the grid of the Stonehenge. I was shown images and numbers beyond my comprehension at the time. I took it all in and was grateful to be there in that moment.

Following the meditation, it took me a few minutes to reconnect and come back to this time-space reality. I loved the energy at Stonehenge; it was comforting, fun, and explorative. It was a place that I did not want to leave. However, we had to begin our journey back to London. I knew deep within me that I would be coming back to this place to further explore. I was not yet done with all the messages it had for me. Therefore, I made

149

an agreement with my Higher Self that I would come back before I left Europe.

On the van ride back, Dmitriy came and sat by me and another traveler named Suha, and we all entered into some deep and fun conversations about what we had experienced at Stonehenge and within life. For the next several hours, on the van ride and then the train ride into London, the three of us shared many laughs and insights. We were all buzzing from the energy of what we had just witnessed and experienced. It was so fun and amazing that we were all sharing the same space. It is a place of unconditional love and compassion. It brings my heart such joy.

We all had different exits on the train into London that night. It felt sad to disconnect from the strong bond we had just created. However, with it being such a unique bond, I knew that we would keep in contact with each other. We immediately formed a group on WhatsApp between us and continued to share our experiences and support each other. It felt beautiful to have such amazing souls with whom I could connect and share. We even added a name to our group: "The Magic Bus." This is what that night felt like. It felt as if we were riding home on a magic bus. We did not have any alcoholic drinks, we were not on any drugs – we were all simply high on life. We were experiencing our true natures and our abilities to be within the flow and feel amazing. Yes, this is what life is about – being the best version of yourself and tapping into that natural ability within yourself after you drop the illusion of who and what you think you are. Thank you, Stonehenge, for reactivating that knowing deep within each of us and allowing us to see ourselves beyond the illusion.

Dmitriy has a magical presence about him. Not only does he have the physical understanding and depth of knowledge around spirituality, but he also truly embarks on the path. I admire the depths of conversations you can reach with him, discussing all sides of the topic. I am grateful for the guidance and alignment that allowed our paths to cross and that we have continued to stay in contact. He has been an inspiration to me, one for which I will be forever grateful.

***

Here is Dmitriy's awakening moment:

My name is Dmitriy, and I am the oldest of two children. Whilst England is not my country of birth, I somehow always knew I would find my home here. Ever since I became aware of this country's existence, I've been drawn to live here. And so, when my parents made the decision to relocate in mid the 90's, it was not a surprise, but yet another confirmation of my earliest observations - there is a perfect timing to everything.

Waking up

At some point in our life, we may experience a moment of extreme clarity – a state of "total awareness." Such a situation can be so significant that it leaves a profound impression on us, potentially changing the course of our entire life.

These types of events bring us in complete alignment with our inner truth. They expand our senses beyond the physical and give us a glimpse of the state of being of our Higher Self. Such an experience can be gently inspired by years of meditation or rapidly created by some life-threatening conditions that jolt us into awakening.

This state of total awareness can also be facilitated by our simply living our lives with joyful optimism while putting our full attention on whatever we're choosing to do – being fully present – here and now. This is a natural way to wake up, and that's exactly what happened with me. Here is my story...

I like to observe my emotions. Since early childhood, I innately understood that feelings were there to direct my attention towards something important, so I would take time during each day to just be still and observe what's going on within. Noticing if I feel balanced or anxious, peaceful or restless, and then exploring the possible reasons for having that experience.

I would often ask myself questions about a situation, and after a short while, answers would come through. The information would simply pop into my mind as something that is just "so obvious." At first, this dialogue was experienced entirely in my mind, a sort of a game that I played with myself. Then, when I actually started writing things down, I found that insights began to really expand and accelerate. In a way, this is what I'm doing here, right now. As I write this, I am focusing my full attention on my journey, and I'm already beginning to get deeper understandings about certain events in my past. This is really exciting!

Let's explore one of the most significant moments of my life that I can recall at present:

I am in high school. It is an "inset" day, which means that there are no classes running but the school is still open so that teachers can prepare for the term ahead. I use this opportunity to come in and catch up on some of my projects. I love the freedom of being able to arrive at a time that suits me, wearing whatever clothes I like, and having access to all the resources of the school without the restrictions of a timetable. I often find that I don't really need any assistance, just a peaceful environment where I can do my own work.

Choosing to come in on an inset day meant that I would essentially have the whole school to myself. Being able to spend several hours focusing on some interesting project completely undisturbed. Working in one classroom, then walking along a quiet, empty corridor to another more relevant space and continuing my work. There might be a few occasions where I would come across a teacher and spend a couple of minutes exchanging pleasantries, but most of the time, it would just be me, completely by myself.

On this particular day, I remember feeling really optimistic – having a sense of knowing that if I stay positively focused on the work at hand, I will be able to complete all the projects before the approaching deadlines. At first, I choose to go to the computer room, picking the most interesting project and giving it my full attention, working on it for several hours without anybody else coming in to disturb me. Then, seeing that I'm making a measurable progress and being pleased with how things are evolving, I decide to take a break and walk across to another part of the school.

As I walk along the corridor, all of a sudden, I feel something. Something completely different. Something that I do not recall ever experiencing before. This change seems so significant that I am drawn to stop right there, in the middle of the corridor.

I stand still, observing what's going on inside and outside of me. The corridor – completely empty, refreshingly cool, dim, and quiet. There is a serene stillness all around me. My body – feeling pleasantly comfortable, there is no pain or discomfort of any kind, and my skin feels like it's being enveloped by gentle softness. I especially notice just how light and comfortable my feet feel, there is absolutely no pressure, as though my body is weightless. My mind – alert yet relaxed, and completely at ease. There are no concerns at all, just peace. Total peace. My heart – feeling a sense of freedom and optimism, filled with excitement, energy, and playful curiosity.

In this moment, I am experiencing a state of complete alignment – a feeling of peace, freedom, and pure unconditional joy.

That experience lasted for a relatively short time, yet it was significant enough to have a profound effect on the rest of my life. From that point forward, I was able to have a full awareness of what true joy feels like, and I knew in my heart that there would come a time when I would able to experience that state on a continuous basis.

I am on that path right now.

12

Care for Wild Rhino Sanctuary, South Africa
Ronald's Awakening Moment

After my adventure in Stonehenge, I had one day to myself before I was scheduled to check out of my place in London. I maybe would have stayed longer, but my hotel was fully booked. I allowed myself time on this day to assimilate all the beauty of what had just transpired and to see where I would go next. I decided to go to yet another sacred site in England: Glastonbury. This is a place where the city was built around several energetic ley lines. I knew that the Glastonbury Abbey was actually on the heart chakra line, and I wanted to stay there. I immediately reached out to them, and, thankfully, they had openings. I originally booked three nights, as that is often what I did for most towns. I usually found that it gave me enough time to explore. However, I ended up extending my stay by an additional three nights, as I fell in love with this unique and fascinating town.

It turned out that guests at the Glastonbury Abbey retreat house had private access to the Glastonbury Abbey itself, via a private gate. This was something I had not known prior but was very pleasantly surprised to learn. In fact, I was beyond excited to know that this was available to me. This allowed me time to explore the energy and connect more deeply. The energy and presence here were delightful. I felt so blessed to be able to do daily meditations here. It was like home.

A unique quality of this town that I found particularly amazing was all the various groups of people that coexist together. I quickly found out that the Glastonbury Abbey retreat house (where I was staying) was still actively used as a Catholic retreat, with service given daily for those wanting to participate. Across the street was a house that advertised services "by witches." Down the other street, there was an ashram led by

Krishnas. Then, when walking down Main Street in town, you would see people dressed as witches, fairies, lords, and all kinds of other costumes. I was in awe at the beauty of how each person expressed him/herself.

One morning, I got up and attended the Catholic reading and service at the retreat house. Then, I walked over to the witch house for an energetic shamanic healing session, which was outstanding. I had lunch in town, and I talked with a few people dressed in fairy costumes. Then, later that evening, I went to a Kirtan chanting event held by the Krishna group. I sat down that night in amazement at the beauty of the day. I am open to all groups of people and all religious beliefs and backgrounds. I consider myself spiritual in nature, and I appreciate many forms of expressing oneself. That is why I ended up extending my stay, as I truly enjoyed the uniqueness of this small town.

Following my stay in Glastonbury, I continued on to Salisbury. From there, I was able to take another day trip back to Stonehenge. Yes, I had promised myself that I would return, and I did. I felt that strong call and intuition to return back to this sacred site, and I listened. This time my visit there was a bit different; since I was on my own, I had time to explore and really sink into the energy present. I still felt the strong buzz of the area. I walked around the whole site until I was guided to where I should engage in mediation. I put down the blanket I had brought with me and went into a deep meditation. Again, I saw images and geometrical patterns that I wrote down, not knowing at that time what they all meant. I was simply thankful for the information I was receiving, knowing it would all make sense when I needed to know.

While I was in this town, two friends and beautiful souls, Megan and Thoryn, whom I had met volunteering at the elephant nature park in Thailand, reached out since they lived close by. Therefore, we met up for dinner one evening. It was so amazing to see them. This was the third country wherein I had crossed paths with them. We met in Thailand, we had been in

Bali at the same time and hiked a mountain together, and now here we were, meeting up again in their home town in England. I loved how life coordinates moments like this. This was not coincidence. Life was bringing us back together again for a higher purpose.

After Salisbury, I went to Bath to experience and soak in the famous hot spas. This was exactly what my body needed at the moment. It provided a perfect balance to allow the experiences of England to integrate and assimilate. Throughout my travels, I was undergoing a big transformation. It was important for me to remember to be gentle with myself and allow myself times to take breaks. This was one of those times.

From Bath, I planned to head up to Scotland. However, I had other friends, whom I had also met at the Elephant Nature Park, who lived in Manchester. Since Manchester was on the way to Edinburgh, I stopped off along the way to visit with them as well. We all had to laugh as it was so funny that I just met up with Megan and Thoryn, and now I was with Lydia and Liam – all people I had met when volunteering at Elephant Nature Park. I was in amazement, as I began my journey with all of them a year ago, and now I was ending my journey with all of them; after Scotland, I had to head back to Michigan. It was like a circle was being completed. I did not know I would see them again when we said goodbye in Thailand, but now here we were.

Lydia and Liam were so much fun. They took me around, and we got to visit Liverpool. I was able to see the home of where the Beatles recorded and played their music. What a trip that was to walk through the history of time. I will forever be grateful for that experience with them.

I had two more stops in the next week and a half before I was to head back. I boarded the train to Edinburgh, Scotland. To my surprise, the Edinburgh festival was going on when I arrived. How lucky was I to be in that town for that exact time, without even planning it? I was able to witness all of the festivities going on along the streets and in the different venues. There were people from all over the world attending this event. One of my highlights was managing to get a last-minute ticket to see the sold-out show of the Edinburgh Military Tattoo. Wow, what an impressive show it was. Hearing the music and seeing the military personnel who had traveled from all around the globe to participate in this event brought tears to my eyes.

My last stop was Findhorn, Scotland. I was guided to this place because I had found out that they had an eco-community. I was fascinated with eco-communities and wanted to be able to live in one for at least a week, in order to experience what life would be like there. I found a place on Airbnb to stay within the local community. The community was amazing. Each house was unique in its own way. Some had grass roofs, some were built from clay and hay bales, some had solar power panels, and some even were built from the foundation of old whiskey barrels. This community was using innovative ways to recycle and reuse.

Within the community, they had a garden, store, local restaurant/café, meditation halls, and a center in which they held classes and events. One of my favorite concepts that I learned from this community was that before each work shift, they would all get together and share how they were doing that day/morning. Therefore, if someone was having a bad day or a rough start, the group knew this and could further support them. Following group sharing, they participated in a group meditation and intention-setting before their work shift began. They also ended their shift in the same manner. What a simple – but genius – idea. This strategy promotes more effective communication so that the workers can support each other, as well as build conscious energy going into the start of each shift. Ultimately, they produce better outcomes as a result.

In the community, they honor everything and everyone. They are aware that everything has a consciousness. This was a blessing to be part of and to witness. Was it all perfect? No, but they were trying the best they knew how, and I could appreciate a different way of approaching living in a true sense of community.

When I left Scotland, it was time to head back to Michigan because my nephew's wedding was coming up in less than two weeks. At this point, it was August of 2017. I had been traveling the globe for almost a year now. It felt very strange to think of going back. Part of me was excited to see family and friends and to be in one place for a few weeks instead of constantly changing locations, but another part of me felt anxious about going back to a place where others did not fully understand the depth of what I was going through. When traveling, I felt like I had a perpetual community, as I would often come across other travelers who were doing the same as I was – exploring the world. There was a sense of understanding without any explanation needed, and no questions were asked. "Where are you going next?" "What are you going to do?" "How are you going to make money?" These would be common questions that the majority of people would want to know – the people that were still grounded in their societal stories.

I tried to be as gentle as possible with myself while coming back, understanding that the shock of reentering the United States and local culture could take time. This is something I was familiar with after traveling many times before. It is a fascinating observation to witness and be a part of. The body becomes easily adapted to the ways of life and customs around it; when you shift that perspective, there can be an adjustment phase. In addition, being back in a familiar environment can trigger old patterns of behavior, even though you may have shifted and grown a new perspective. These are the beautiful moments that travel can bring, allowing you to shed those parts of yourself that no longer serve your highest and greatest good. What amazing gifts that I was embarking on.

The wedding of my nephew, Ryan, and his fiancée, Rachel, was coming up quickly, and I wanted to put the last-minute touches on their ceremony. Right before I left in November of

2016, they had asked me if I would perform their ceremony. I was deeply honored and told them that no matter where I was in the world, I would come home for their wedding. I would not miss it. I had written down many notes over the past few months as I got inspiration for the big day. It was such a special day to be part of, to witness, and to share in my nephew starting a new chapter in his life with Rachel, who was such a beautiful soul. I felt very blessed to take part in such a special occasion.

It was also a time of celebration. There were family and relatives that came in from all around the States, some whom I had not seen in quite some time. It was a reunion of family. After being gone for a year, it was beautiful to be able to see and reconnect with so many of them on the wedding day and throughout the following week.

After visiting with friends and family for about a month, I knew deep down that it was time to go again. Some asked if (and some had assumed that) I would now head to California, as I had been planning a year prior. However, I was being guided to travel again. It was not yet the right time to find a permanent place to stay. During my meditations, it was clear that I still needed to visit a few more places, two of which were South Africa and Costa Rica. These were two destinations that I had wanted to visit for several years. The time was now, so I decided I would head out on Part Two of Rob's World Adventure.

However, before I was guided out of the country, there were a few places in the United States that I wanted to visit. Traveling the globe, I realized that we often do not even see some of the beauty in our own backyard. I had been to quite a few of the states over the years, but there were still some destinations that I was really being guided to. These destinations included Yosemite National Park and Santa Fe, New Mexico.

Therefore, I met my spirit sister, Candace, in California, and together we drove to Yosemite. The day we drove into the actual park, I was almost in tears at the awe and beauty of nature I was witnessing. It was like a postcard. The famous Yosemite picture

I had seen many times before was now standing right before me. I was overwhelmed with gratitude to be able to experience that moment.

Following Yosemite, my next stop was Santa Fe. There was an Earthship community just north of there in Taos that I have wanted to visit and check out for some time. My friends, Tina and Julie, met me there and we drove in together. I looked into Airbnb, as I really wanted to stay in an Earthship. To my wonderment, there was one available during the time I was looking. It was surreal to be able to stay within an Earthship overlooking the New Mexico dessert and night sky. The house was built halfway down in the ground, which kept it cool all year round at a constant temperature. It had solar panels for electricity and a four-tier water system which recycled the water from the sink so that it then flowed to the toilet and plants. It was such a phenomenal design. The walls were made of recycled tires and bottles. The home felt comfortable and grounding. It warmed my heart to see a whole community of houses being built with recycled material and eco-conscious living. Some of the houses looked like they were from another universe in the design. It was truly fantastic.

After our adventure, we drove to Colorado to visit our other spirit sister, Tanya. We all came together to do a mini CranioSacral Therapy intensive with each other. We had done this before, and it was amazing. I felt blessed to have such close friends and colleagues with whom I could get together and do this. It is so important that we all get our own work done and coming together in this fashion really allows us to dive deep within and clear through many of our own boundaries in a supportive space. It was a beautiful time to integrate the journey I was on, as well as the one I was about to go back into. I have such a deep passion and love for the work that I do with CranioSacral Therapy. It has been such an effective tool to allow myself to progress forward in life with more ease, and to see and let go of the old stories/paradigm.

Following this deep work, I was ready to explore the next three places I was being guided to. While I was planning for South Africa, my friends, Anthony and Mary reached out and told me that they were going to Mauritius. They had invited me several times over the years, but I had always been unable to go. Well, this time I was free, and I said yes. In fact, it worked out perfectly – when I looked on a map, I learned that Mauritius was right next to South Africa, where I wanted to go next. Therefore, we rented a house, and I left Colorado and headed to Mauritius for a month. Since they had been there many times before, they showed me around the island. One of the highlights that they offered on their retreats in the past was to swim with dolphins in the ocean and do CranioSacral Therapy while walking with lions, both of which I wanted to experience.

I had noticed something deep within me shifting over the past year. Since I worked with the rescued elephants in Thailand, I had this calling and deep desire to work with more large animals doing CranioSacral Therapy. This is what was guiding me here to Mauritius and South Africa. Being back in the ocean with the dolphins in their home was exhilarating. Each time, I got that buzzing sensation within my cells. Mary was feeling this as well, as we had just had a small pod swim right up to us as we entered the ocean. The two of us laughed hysterically when we got back onto the boat, as we were both in such a state of bliss. The sound vibrations that the dolphins emit are so powerful. I was on a high the rest of the day from this energy, reconnecting and remembering the pure energy that we all are.

Later in the week, we went to the place where we were able to get in and walk with lions. I had conflicting energy before entering. The lions were in a large enclosure. I knew that they had been rescued and were being rehabilitated, but I thought that they should be in the wild. A few guides shared with us that after being in captivity, it is hard for them to be released back into the wild. This was something that I was going to be exploring over the next few months: *what is "the wild?"* The guides appeared to really love the animals, and vice versa. I had to tune into my role and what was guiding me here. I could offer these giant beings the loving touch of CranioSacral Therapy to further assist with their healing and wellbeing; therefore, that is what I did. As I walked alongside or crouched next to them, I gently yet firmly placed a hand on their backs or stroked their spines. I did so with the loving intention of the work for their highest and greatest good. It was amazing to witness their CranioSacral rhythms and how they would respond. They would often let out a purr, or you could see their body postures relax. It was surreal to be able to work with such beautiful beings. What a gift. It taught me to maintain a whole new sense of neutral, being beside a large lion. Thank you for such a phenomenal lesson.

After working with the lions and as well as cheetahs, it stirred up a bunch of questions within me. *"What was happening within me? Is there a 'wild' left? Has man taken over the land such that we have left no room for the animals to be free in what was once their home?"* No animal should be caged; they should be allowed to roam free. Is it humane to train and ride horses? Some say, "Well, our ancestors did." Just because they did, does that make it right? *"No,"* I thought to myself. *"Horses should be allowed to roam free, too – not ridden by people as pets, or on vacation at the beach, or on a trail trekking through the mountain."* Who says we can take their freedom? Are *we* actually free? Or are we in our own cage, a cage called society? This is what was stirring in my head as I was working and experiencing time with these animals.

Originally, I had thought that I wanted to go to Mauritius just to have fun and to be with the animals, and then go to South Africa to experience a safari and see animals in their natural habitat. I did not anticipate or imagine this deep process I was embarking on as it stirred within my soul. I was being guided here for a reason – a reason I did not fully understand at the time but was slowly coming to understand now.

As I mentioned, I had initially wanted to go on a safari in South Africa. However, as I was looking into the many options offered, something did not feel right. I knew something was not aligning. I had approximately less than a week left before I was supposed to leave for Africa, but something was missing. Then one day, as I did a new search for safaris in Africa, I came across an option that allowed travelers to volunteer with the animals. This was it; this was the missing link. I had done this in Thailand and loved it. I wanted to give back to Africa and to the animals. However, which one should I choose? There were some options that would allow me to work with tiger cubs, but again, something was not right about that. Then I came across a website that offered visitors the opportunity to work with orphaned rhinos. This sanctuary cared for young rhinos whose mothers had been poached. I immediately sent the company a message to see if they had openings in a week's time, and they told me they did. This was where I needed to be. I had never imagined myself working with rhinos, but this felt so right. I realized again that when I align myself to my highest and greatest good (and then get any expectations of what that should look like out of the way), that I am then guided to the exact right place at the exact right time.

I arrived in Johannesburg, South Africa, and took the bus to the meeting spot where the company was going to pick me up. The owners that organized the volunteers to work with the rhinos were so inspiring and amazing. They had such a passion for educating others on the crisis that was occurring. As we arrived at Care for Wild Africa, I sat back in awe at what I was about to experience. They told me that the site had to be protected, as rhino horns were in demand on the black market. Therefore, you had to pass through three security gates to get inside the compound. Once inside, you could see ex-military patrolling the grounds to make sure the rhinos stayed safe. Wow, I had no idea. I had imagined that going to work with rescued rhinos would be similar to working with the elephants in Thailand. I had no clue what was really happening in South Africa or what I was about to encounter.

As soon as I met all the staff that worked there, it felt like home. Another volunteer stationed in my same department told me, "You have to meet Ronald; he is the rhino whisperer." Ronald was in the first department where they scheduled me to work. He had such a natural calmness with each individual rhino. From the moment I met him, he always had a smile on his face and emitted a joyful presence. I could tell that the rhinos understood this as well, as they clearly shared a mutual respect. The symbiotic relationship they had with each other was such a beautiful thing to witness firsthand. This is why I was guided to Care for Wild Africa.

I was there for ten days. Volunteering and working with the rhinos was no easy job – it was very physical and labor-intensive, but also so rewarding. There were four departments in which to work: the ICU with the youngest babies that just arrived, the two different places where the rhinos would be moved to once they got a bit older, and, finally, the enclosures of all the other rescued animals that were there. The other animals included a hippo, lion, and many smaller species. I began my volunteer time in the two areas for the older rhinos. Our duties included bottle feeding in the morning and afternoon, cleaning up their bomas (houses), sweeping, washing the floors in their enclosures, shoveling lots and lots of poop, and getting their other food (hay and pellets) ready. We also did various side jobs as time allowed, in order to assist with the upkeep of the place. Overseeing the care of these rhinos was a large operation to run.

There was one particular event that happened during my time there that I will never forget. It was my second day there. My fellow volunteers and I went into the large area where most of rhinos lived so that we could shovel up the massive number of poop piles. While most of the rhinos stay in this area at night, during the day they are free to roam the hillside since they are supervised by the guards. Therefore, this area was empty that day, except for three rhinos that were being monitored due to showing some signs of illness. The other workers warned me that I should always keep one eye out to see where the rhinos were while we were in this space, so I did. As the group walked in, the curious rhinos came over to check out the tractor. As I was shoveling and keeping my eye on the rhinos, one of them decided to charge and run at me. I immediately dropped my shovel and ran in the opposite direction, as I had been instructed to do. The rhino stopped quickly, as he was more curious about my shovel on the ground. However, my heart was racing, and I realized the capacity of who I was working with. These were still animals with instinctual behaviors and curiosities, and they could easily harm us with their weight and strength. After I regained my composure, I laughed with the others. We said that it must have been a part of my initiation; since I survived, I was now welcome to the club.

During my time there, I rotated through each of the four departments because I asked to experience all of them. Several days after I arrived, I went to the ICU. The smaller babies were so adorable. The youngest was two months old. It was tragic to read their charts about how they ended up there. All of their mothers had been killed, poached for their horns. I later found out that on the black market, a rhino horn was worth more than gold or drugs/cocaine. This was astonishing. To my further surprise, I also learned that China and Taiwan were the two main countries involved in the corruption of trying to obtain rhino horns. Their motives stemmed from two cultural beliefs. Number one: displaying a rhino horn in your home was a status factor that indicated great wealth. Number two: their people believed that rhino horns served as both a cure for cancer as well as an aphrodisiac – both of which are false.

Rhinos are becoming an endangered species. The extremes poachers go to just to obtain these horns are heart-wrenching. Killing an innocent rhino in order to shave off both of its horns, all the way down to the skin on its nose, and for what? Power? Money? Greed? When the attacked rhino is a mother, this then leaves an orphaned baby by itself – a baby that will stay by the mom even though she has been killed. If the authorities do not hear the gunshot or find the baby rhino within twenty-four hours, it will likely fall prey to another animal. What is wrong with humans? How do some people get to this point? These were the types of questions that were being sparked within me.

To add another level of depth to this tragedy, I found out that often, there are levels of corruption behind the poaching. The top men making the orders often find a lower-income person in Africa and promise them an equivalent of four years' salary (or more) for just one kill. If this lower-income individual is caught, the men who hired him are still free. Not only that, but there is reason to believe that some airport security personnel are in on this deal, as that is likely how the poachers smuggle the horns through customs. The levels of corruption were mind-boggling to me.

I slowly felt rage and anger building inside of me as I heard all of this, but I knew that was not the solution. Anger and rage only create more of that. What could I do instead? I could do exactly what I was doing. I was volunteering, assisting (even if only in a small way) this amazing organization, giving love and CranioSacral touch to the rhinos as often as I could while bottle-feeding, and educating others on what was happening. I had not previously known what was occurring, but I could now educate others through my experience. Knowledge is key. I understand why I was guided to this phenomenal organization.

When I left Care for Wild Africa, I had a new spark and passion within me. I was trying to do the best I could, and knew my role was that of an educator – to share with others through my own personal experiences. I will be forever grateful for being guided to this phenomenal facility, as well as for having met Ronald.

Ronald truly embodies living in the moment, appreciating all that he encounters. His ability to connect with the rhinos is truly remarkable, as he appears one with the group. Ronald displays a sense of enthusiasm and ease with all his interactions.

***

Here is Ronald's awakening moment:

Sanibona, my name is Ronald. I am from Mpumalanga in South Africa. I am a young man who is always keen to help. My greatest thanks goes to my parents, who brought me into this world, for all of their support.

My deepest appreciation goes to Good Work Foundation and Petronel Nieuwoudt for giving me the chance to be exposed to the wildlife.

I am working at Care for Wild Rhino Sanctuary as an animal attendant. I work with the rhinos. I have a special connection with rhinos. The relationship that I have with rhinos is unique - it just flows within me. I am in love with the rhinos. I have a big respect for our wildlife. Now I am referred to as the rhino whisperer.

The place where I am from is very close to the Kruger National Park, and whenever I am reading the news, I always see that rhinos have been poached in the Kruger National Park, on the side that is nearest to my place. Then I told myself that the rhinos that are still alive; I will help them not to become extinct so that our future generations can see what is a rhino, and to see a rhino in its natural habitat.

I was about seventeen years old when I told myself that, one day, I will try my best to save these animals. At this same age, I was in high school (secondary school), studying agricultural sciences, geography and life sciences. It was more about the nature.

As I completed my high school, I went to study at Good Work Foundation. It is a program for local youth. I was studying FGASA (Field Guide's Association of Southern Africa) Nature Guiding. As I was studying, the love for nature and to protect our animals grew so big within me.

167

In 2016, we came to volunteer for two weeks at Care for Wild Rhino Sanctuary, as a group from the Good Work Foundation. Then I saw the great work that Care for Wild Rhino Sanctuary is doing to save the orphan rhinos. Then I told Petronel (the founder) of Care for Wild Rhino Sanctuary that I want to work here, and luckily she said, "after your graduation comes." That's how I came to work here.

As I started working with rhinos at Care for Wild Rhino Sanctuary, my life completely changed. Every time, when I work with the rhinos, I tell myself that these baby rhinos we have here I still want to see them in thirty years in their natural habitat. Whenever I am with the rhinos, there is the natural flow within me. I have a big respect for them. They are very special for us. Day after day, they teach me how to work with them. I can work with baby rhinos, young adults and also adult rhinos, in an excellent way.

The relationship that I have with rhinos sometimes makes me think that I am not a human, I am a rhino, because I never thought that rhinos can love humans because of what cruel people are doing to them. But lucky enough they love me, they feel more protected when I am around them, they feel safe. These are the reasons why people are calling me the rhino whisperer.

Care for Wild has the vision that the whole world must have, to save all the rhinos that are still remaining so that our future generations can experience and know a rhino. I will always support Care for Wild's vision.

I dedicated my life to save rhinos. I wish everyone in the world can have the same mind to save our rhinos which God has given to us, to look after them, because they are also part of the nature that was given to us in the beginning to look after. Then let us all stand together and save our rhinos. Think of our future generations, think of our nature, think of our poor rhinos. I love rhinos; can you please love them too?

13

Nosara, Costa Rica
Dustin's Awakening Moment

After I finished volunteering with the rhinos, I headed off for a four-day safari at the famous Kruger National Park. This had been a dream of mine for years. However, the reality of it turned into so much more than I had ever expected. I made arrangements to stay within Kruger National Park itself, and each day we would go for drives through the park. I had set this up through Working with Rhinos; you could add it on before or after your trip if you wanted to. The first day that we started out on our Jeep safari, we found out that another rhino had been poached the night before. Not only that, but it turned out that this rhino had been poached by one of the resort workers. It was part of the corruption again. To my even greater surprise, I learned that the head of the anti-poaching unit within Kruger National Park had been arrested months earlier for being involved with the corruption as well. What? The head of anti-poaching was in on it, too?

Getting to be in nature and driving around in an-open air safari truck was like a dream come true. Our guide was great. She explained to us that we were in the wild, and whatever animals we happened to come across would be the ones that we saw on any given day. This was not the zoo. I was finally able to see animals in their true and natural habitat, roaming free as they should be. This is what I thought, at least.

It turned out that they were as free as they could be. There were still fences around Kruger National Park, though it would take days to drive from one side of the park to the other. I learned that they have a committee that is in charge of population control. This is mostly for the elephants, as they are overpopulated. We were told that when elephants are overpopulated, they destroy trees/bushes/nature that houses

169

other species, and then those other animals die. Therefore, their solution to manage this was to kill off some of the elephants in the park. What? When did humans become the deciders of who was going to live and die? This was the animals' home. This was the free safari, so I had thought. This was the one place where they were supposed to be able to live as nature intended. As I moved deeper into the safari and learned more, more deep thoughts were stirring within me.

I enjoy learning about everything that goes on behind the scenes of the places I visit, but it can also be very difficult to integrate. I came to the conclusion that, ultimately, there is no "wild" left. This was as close to living "wild" as the animals could get. Most free lands have been populated and dominated by humans. This park was humans' attempt at living in harmony with nature. I agree it was much better than a zoo, where they cage animals for display, education, and enjoyment. I was fortunate to witness the efforts of many who were still advocates for the animals, ultimately trying to find a better balance.

During my four days there, I was privileged to see giraffes eating from the trees, elephant herds roaming off in the distance protecting their young, and lions perched on the rocks in the distance. This was the animal kingdom. Thank you for allowing me to come into your home for a few days to be part of it.

Following the safari, I knew I wanted to head down to the garden route to Cape Town, so I flew to Port Elizabeth. While in Port Elizabeth, I spotted an advertisement for a safari within a privately-owned park. Having just left a national, government-owned park, I was curious to witness the difference. So, I went right back into another three-day safari. The privately-owned parks were smaller in size, but still large. You could often see "the big five" all within just a few hours, as the drivers knew where the animals usually hung out. At this park, one of the lions had just had cubs. They told us that the lion cubs would be sold; since it was a small park, there could only be one dominant male. That is when I began to see the differences within the privately-owned parks. They said that they would sell the cubs to another park, and since they wanted a hippo, they would trade for or purchase that. This was a very strange concept to me: selling and buying animals. They appeared to be very well looked-after, and they were able to roam free within the park's land. They were not fed; it was nature, and they were part of the circle of life. On two of the drives, I actually witnessed a lion and a tiger hunt and kill a deer. Moments like these – when I was in nature, witnessing the natural habits of animals – are precious to me. I felt blessed to be able to witness and see the difference between the two park environments. Each was unique in its own way, offering me gifts so that could further my growth on this path.

As I worked my way down the garden route, I saw an opportunity to do a shark cage dive. I had seen a friend post pictures of this type of adventure on social media a year prior, and it had sparked an interest with me. It was another opportunity to be up close with a large animal that I would never otherwise be able to, so of course I signed up. The day we went out, the ocean was a bit rough, and we waited for over four hours with no sign of sharks.

Since we did not see any sharks after four hours, we headed back to shore. Once we got back, the guides offered us the chance to go back out again later that day or to sign up for another time (pending availability) since we did not see a shark on our excursion. I wanted to see a shark, so I hurried to the counter to inquire, and learned that they had two openings on a boat that was leaving in just fifteen minutes. I, along with a friend that I had met on the first boat, tried our luck a second time. This time, we were only out on the water for about twenty minutes before sharks started to come to the boat. The crew put out the cage that we would use to enter the water. I slowly entered the cage with both fear and excitement running through me, as right before I entered I saw a shark surface with his mouth open. As I was dangling in the cage, like open bait, the guy above yelled, "Shark!" to signal to us that he was coming. At that moment, I submerged myself in the freezing cold waters and looked straight ahead. Wow!! This shark was heading directly for those of us in the cage, with his mouth open. I could see right into this mouth. I was eye-to-eye with a great white shark. What a powerful moment that was when we locked eyes. He showed such strength and force. That was a moment I will never forget. He was sharing with me the gift that he carries. His mouth grabbed onto the bars of the cage right in front of me. What an exhilarating moment!

As I made my way out of the cage after he swam away so that the next group could enter, I knew something magical had just happened. Never before could I have imagined that I would someday be face-to-face with a great white shark. It was a priceless and life-changing moment. A little bit later, I entered the cage one more time, and had another opportunity to observe and witness this amazing creature swim around me. I was on a high the rest of the day. Thank you, great white shark, for sharing your wisdom and beauty. I was guided here for those gifts.

I finished the rest of the garden route drive down to Cape Town, South Africa. Along the way, I was able to bungee jump again off a bridge crossing. This marked my fourth time bungee jumping in the past year. I was living my dreams and following the guidance of my heart. By the time I reached Cape Town, I knew it would soon be time to head to Costa Rica. Costa Rica was a country that I had talked about going to for several years. Up until that point, it had not been the right time yet; however, now it was calling.

I wanted to go to Costa Rica for many reasons. For one, I had met a friend named Sierra on our blog talk radio show that was doing dolphin swims in the Costa Rican ocean, and I wanted to partake. Therefore, Drake Bay was my first stop upon entering the country. I knew this area was a biodiverse region that was home to many dolphin species. The day had come. I was beyond excited. It was amazing to finally meet Sierra in person after

172

years of contact. During this ocean adventure, there were so many dolphin species playing, jumping, and spinning for us. In all the other times I had been blessed to swim with dolphins in other parts of the world, I had never seen so many in one spot. There were hundreds of dolphins, in all directions.

Sierra was very in tune with the dolphins' energy and showed the utmost respect for them. We cruised along with the pods for over twenty minutes, making sure the dolphins wanted to interact with us before we got in the water. Then, the moment would come. Sierra offered a very unique way of swimming with the dolphins. On the other tours I had been on, they had allowed us in the water two at a time. We had snorkel gear, and we would swim using only our hands, as kicking often startles the dolphins. The dolphins swam so fast you would only have brief moments of sight and interactions. However, on Sierra's tour, there were small handles tied onto each side of the boat. The boat slowed down just enough for two of us to get into the water with our snorkel gear, one on each side of the boat, holding onto the handles. The boat would then continue to cruise along, and the dolphins would continue to play with the boat. Since I was holding onto to the handle as the boat cruised along, I felt as if I was within the pod. I had tears rolling down my face, as it was such a surreal moment. As I looked down towards the ocean floor, there was nothing but a wall of dolphins below me. They were also swimming next to me and in front of me. I was literally swimming in the middle of the pod. It was unlike anything I had ever experienced before. I was in true bliss. I have always had a love for dolphins and their amazing ability to use sonar frequencies to communicate and heal. I will be forever grateful for that experience.

I loved my experience so much that I planned a second trip. However, while we were able to see dolphins swimming in the distance on the second trip, the sea conditions were rough. Therefore, we were unable to get in the water with them. Nevertheless, I was grateful to be out on the water and within

173

their energy field. To witness dolphin play and swim together is such a beauty.

My next stop was Finca Bellavista, a tree house community near Golfito, Costa Rica. This was another place that I had come across years prior and had wanted to visit ever since, due to my love of tree houses. I have had visions of opening a fun tree house community retreat center for quite some time. Therefore, coming here to see and live in a tree house was a dream. I had been in contact with the owners over the years, and I had seen that they had a few for sale at this time. I wanted to check it out, maybe even with the possibility of moving.

Walking through this treehouse community was like being in a fairytale. There was a basecamp community area, in which they had a dining hall, yoga area, and room to hang out. They had three tree houses/villas right next to base camp for those that could not hike to the others, as getting to the next closest tree house required at least a fifteen-minute hike across a suspension bridge and up, down, and around some moderate trails through the jungle. Yes, you were definitely immersed in nature here.

My tree house that I rented for the week was about a twenty-minute hike to base camp. From my house, you could hear the waterfall that was down below in the distance. Being in that home was so peaceful and relaxing. There was a family of bats that lived outside but hung upside down on the screen from the window of the shower. They were so adorable. The other treehouses in the community ranged in size from cozy studios to giant mansions in the trees, each stunning in their own ways. The community also had its own garden, wherein they grew most of their food.

Each day, I went for a hike, walked along the river, swam in the waterfalls, visited with the other guests that I met, and was able to journal, read, and get into some very deep meditations. I really enjoyed living in a treehouse, as it made me feel very childlike and playful. My only disappointment with this

174

community was that it was not the "community" that I had anticipated. There were close to twenty treehouses in the community; however, only two couples lived there full-time. Those two couples were the ones that ran the property. I was told that the others only come a few times a year, if that, and rent out their place the rest of the time. I had the idea that this was a community in which everyone lived but having the majority of them as rentals did not create a community-like environment. Therefore, buying a treehouse here, like I had originally had thought, was not what I wanted after all. However, I was grateful I had the opportunity to experience such a unique gift. I was guided here to take away some ideas and visions for the future.

Another vision I'd had for my trip to Costa Rica was to immerse myself in a Spanish class. I had taken an introductory course a few years back, but I really wanted to learn more. One of the couples I met at the treehouse community had just come from an eco-village near Arenal. I checked it out and discovered that they had openings to stay in the village, as well as a Spanish immersion class. At first I planned to stay there for two weeks, but I ended up cutting my visit down to just one week because the weather was not ideal. Each day it rained and was chilly. There were nights that I slept while wearing both my jacket and hat. The owners of the place I was staying understood and were kind enough to give me a refund for my second week.

I wanted sunshine and warm weather when I left, so I headed to the Guanacaste coast. I came across Envision Festival, which offered yoga, music, and health talks. This event was coming up in less than three weeks' time. When I looked into tickets, I saw an option to volunteer. They were offering a deal where you could take a course on herbal first aid medicine for the week prior to the festival and then volunteer by learning how to set up a pop-up first aid clinic and helping run it at the festival. I had used herbal medicine throughout the years, but I wanted to learn more as it had always fascinated me. *"This is such a perfect opportunity and perfect timing,"* I thought. I reached out to them and learned that they still had openings. I was so excited about all of the amazing gifts and offerings that Costa Rica was presenting to me – the dolphins, the tree house community, Spanish lessons, and now, to my surprise, an opportunity to learn more about herbal medicine. All of the previous opportunities had been things that I had envisioned doing ahead of time when I first planned to come to Costa Rica. However, this herbal clinic aligned completely unexpectedly. I knew from experience that those unexpected gifts can be the greatest discoveries.

I had two weeks before the class started, so I took the opportunity to explore the many beach towns along the pacific coast. It was so happy to be in warm weather and sun again. This served as a reminder to myself of how much I truly appreciated this type of climate and what a difference it made on my overall wellbeing. I realized that when I eventually looked for a place to settle back down, warm weather and sun would be two very important factors to me.

When I headed to this area, my sister's friend, Stephanie (who was following my travels via social media), told me that her parents lived along the coast and put me in contact with them. Debbie and Ben reached out to me, and in just a few days I was staying at their gorgeous house. I loved how things align so perfectly. I had not seen them since I was a very young child, and it was so nice to sleep in a family house for a few nights. I really began to appreciate the small things of a nice bed, my own room, running water, hot water, and clean towels. I had been traveling around the globe for quite a while now, and I had lived in many conditions.

I almost did not want to leave the comforts of such a nice house. However, I had already made reservations to stay in yet another eco-community before I had to make my way to the Caribbean side of the island for the herbal medicine class. Therefore, I headed to PachaMama. I had discovered this place a few months prior when a friend of mine had shared with me how much he had enjoyed his time there. Since I was in the area and exploring different eco-communities, I decided to check it out.

The day I arrived. They were just starting a clarity breath work class for the week. I looked into attending, but it had already started and was full. I figured it was just as well, since the reason I was there was to check out this new way of living. I had my own open-air bungalow with a mosquito net over the bed and shared bathrooms and showers. It was quite amazing, as my bungalow was about a twenty-minute hike into the jungle from the base community. I did appreciate the remoteness of the rooms and the chance to be engulfed in nature.

At PachaMama, they offered different workshops and cleanses. Unfortunately, however, the dates for the classes did not work out with the time I was there. There were others, like myself, who were not in a workshop and instead just enjoying the peace of the community. They had a dining hall with fresh organic foods prepared each day that were delicious. They also offered an "elixir bar," which became one of my favorite amenities in the community. I loved this concept. Instead of offering alcohol, which was not allowed within the community, they offered fresh, organic, herbal drinks that promoted health and wellness. This totally resonated with me.

As with other communities I had visited, there were highlights that I enjoyed and other aspects that I did not care for. I did not resonate with the complete energy of the community as a whole. I also learned, after attending some of the events, that I did not resonate with the founder of the place, either. During my time there, I learned that they held special ceremonies a few times a month during which they offered a drink made from a form of ayahuasca. I appreciated being able to witness this within myself, as it was really aiding me in becoming clear on what I wanted for the future. If I did not have this exploration, I would not have known exactly what was working for me or not.

This was not. I was looking for a community that did not rely on outside substances to gain insight.

Two days before my reservation ended, I was attending a yoga chant class. I came across an individual named Dustin. Dustin had just arrived the day prior. Following class, we got into some great conversations about life. I shared with him my experiences and what I was going through. He provided me with a different insight, as he had been to PachaMama before and now he had returned to do another cleanse. I realized that your time here could be very different if you were engaged in a program that served as the purpose for your trip.

The next day, Dustin and I continued our conversations about health and what had brought him to PachaMama for the cleanse. Our conversation gave me new insight into the effects that prescribed pharmaceuticals have on our bodies. As we all know, prescribed medications are given to people for various reasons – anxiety, depression, sleep disorders, pain, etc. When taken for an extended period of time, however, they can cause neurological symptoms. My conversation with Dustin deepened my inspiration to work further with medicinal plants to help find a natural solution and alternative for people. I was so grateful Dustin crossed my path at that moment. He was providing me with a new depth and insight to spark inspiration within me.

As I was having breakfast on the day I left, Dustin asked if he could come with me to Nosara. He suggested that he only come for the day; he had to come back that night, as his program was starting the next day. I thought, *"How perfect! It will be fun to hang out with him more and explore a new town with someone I know."* Another friend I met there, Pam, decided to join us as well. She would also just come for the day, as she was going to be in the same cleanse program as Dustin. Therefore, the three of us headed into the next town: Nosara.

I immediately fell in love. It was such a drastic shift in energy from where I had been. This place showed the true meaning of a community. It was a small beach town with a lot of individuals who surfed and did yoga, which attracted a mindset that was more in alignment with my own values and interests. While I was in this town, I kept running into people that I had met in my travels either earlier in Costa Rica or who had been at PachaMama, too. It felt as if it were a little vortex. Dustin, Pam, and I enjoyed our day at the beach, laughing and having fun. I told them I would be there for almost a week if they wanted to come back and join me after their class. To my surprise, they both came back two days later for the weekend, as they had a two-day break between their class and the cleanse. It was super fun to reunite and hang out all weekend.

When they left a second time, I knew that I would see them again at some point in the future. In just a short time, we had developed such a special bond among the three of us. It turned out that Dustin and I would again cross paths in less than two months, when I came back to the United States.

I honor Dustin for his strength and the courage that he displays. He is devoted to a new path of health and wellness for himself. Dustin demonstrates an openness to exploration that is beautiful to witness. I am grateful that our paths crossed in Costa Rica and that we continue to stay in contact. I know I was guided to PachaMama to unite with him and spark something deep within myself – a new awakening and exploration. Thank you, Dustin, for those gifts.

***

Here is Dustin's awakening moment:

Hi, my name is Dustin. I was born in Gaithersburg, Maryland. I grew up in a very rural part of Maryland. I have two older brothers, and both my parents are still here to this day. My childhood was quite interesting from the beginning. My extended family is all in the automotive business together, which has created a toxic environment. Growing up in that type of environment, it was always about one-

upping the other family members and using the children as pawns against each other.

It was a competition of who was better at sports, who was better at school, and what degree you got. This all led to unhealthy behaviors within the family. Along with the dynamics of the family, I barely knew my father growing up. He was absolutely consumed with work and with making my brother into a professional racecar driver. He worked twelve hours per day, came home and I would barely see him, and on the weekends he was off doing anything to do with my brother's career. I spent a lot of my life in a kind of single-parent household. My mother has been battling her own demons since she was a kid. I spent most of my life with a very depressed, negative, and, at times, abusive mother.

I made it through high school but lacked a lot of self-confidence most of my childhood and into college. My past, with the way I was raised and everything going on, made me feel like I did not have an option of what to do. So I became what they knew. I went to a well-known college within my family and got a scholarship there. I went on to get the engineering degree that I was expected to, even though I did not enjoy the subject matter. I struggled through college quite a bit because it did not feel right for me. It felt like I was going along with what I was supposed to do. During that time, I was having unbelievable sleeping problems. I never found out why I had them – I just took the medicine I was given even though it made me feel horrible. After graduation, the only thing I wanted to do was go into the military to fly. However, a shoulder surgery disqualified me for a couple years. So I ended up being an energy-efficient engineer for the Navy at the Pentagon.

I excelled massively in this position, just like most things I have tried. I was making more money than most of my friends who had graduated college. However, I was absolutely miserable. During this time, I was continuing to have massive sleeping problems. My sleep was very sporadic; it wasn't uncommon for me to go three to five days without sleep. Everything I was working for and felt I had to do had led me to a place where I was miserable. I was lost. I did not know *what to do. I tried to please those around me. I thought this is what I had to do the rest of my life. It left me feeling depressed.*

I found myself in a very dark place, so my brother reached out to me and wanted me to talk to someone who lived in PachaMama. This person left his whole successful life in LA and went to PachaMama. During this whole time, from college up until this point, I was treated for the symptoms of not sleeping with a pharmaceutical. While on this medication, no doctor ever tried to figure out the cause of what was happening. The medication helped me to sleep but made me feel miserable during the daytime.

I got the information, took a leap, and went down to PachaMama, Costa Rica, with the commitment of one month. I arrived in Costa Rica, coming from a super conservative background and working in the Navy, and now showing up to this hippy place that appeared like a commune. When I first arrived, I wanted to leave immediately. But the longer I stayed, the more my eyes opened to a different lifestyle – a different way to live life. I was showered with support. People generally appeared to care about my well-being. I did not know how to accept this. I did not know how to accept these people's love. I was getting very emotional. All the conventions of my life beliefs were being ripped apart.

Even though it was an amazing experience, I still listened to my family. They said that if I did not come back by Christmas, I would pretty much be disowned. So I cut my trip short and came back. However, I did take some of the lessons from PachaMama to heart. I was eating healthier, doing some yoga, and generally was just happier. Since I could not go to the military again, I decided to go fly on my own. I moved to Florida and proceeded to get my private pilot's license for helicopters. I only really planned to get one license, and then probably have to move back to Maryland. I ended up doing so well that I was picked out of flight school by a company, and I proceeded to work for the company in exchange for two more licenses, including my commercial helicopter rating. This started a run of four years total, flying and working for an aerial filming company.

I absolutely love flying, but I was having a difficult time keeping up with the pace of the job due to still not sleeping. I lost several friends during the course of the time I was flying due to sleep deprivation. They lost their lives due to lack of sleep, which caused night crashes and other accidents. I accepted the fact that I could go at any moment, but I didn't feel comfortable with the idea of injuring someone due to the fact I was rarely fully rested.

Eventually, after a few stops and a few other jobs, I ended back up in Maryland, as I took a job in engineering. I ended back up in the same toxic environment. I was still not sleeping. I tried everything this time to figure out what was causing the sleep problems. Over the years, I tried changing my diet, exercise, supplements, etc. At the end of this whole thing, I was back in a place that I did not want to be and was unhealthy to me. I listened to my family once again and went to see yet another doctor. He guaranteed to me that he could get me to sleep. I was so unbelievably desperate that I went to the doctor, we talked, and I started on his protocol to get me to sleep.

What I didn't know was that it was going to throw me down the worst experience of my life. It almost killed me.

The first few weeks/months of the protocol were great. I would take my medicine about thirty minutes before bed, fall asleep, and wake up six to eight hours later. I never really felt fully rested, but it was way better than what I was used to. About two and a half months later, something really odd started happening. I never really had anxiety before, but out of the blue I started to have massive amounts of anxiety and it would only go away when I would take my medicine at night. As I was checking in with my doctor, he suggested that we up the dose, which I gladly concurred with because I was still under the impression that this "amazing" doctor who worked at NIH for forty years knew what he was doing. Well, a few weeks went by, and now I wasn't having anxiety – I was having full-blown panic attacks, and it was affecting my work and my life horribly. I would barely get through an incredibly stressful day at work, go home, and take my medicine so I could feel better. I checked in with my doctor again, and this time he said I should take another long-acting medication during the day because I most certainly had an anxiety disorder. I, once again, listened to my doctor and started taking the new medication, even though I was confused about how I could have developed such bad anxiety so quickly. Even the pharmacists were hesitant to fill my prescriptions because they thought it was abnormal.

So, I kept this program up for some time, until I realized that something was incredibly wrong. I was taking so many pills, and if I didn't take them, I would start to feel horrible. I am not talking about feeling slightly bad; I am talking about feeling like at any moment I would keel over. I would sweat profusely, my heart would beat as fast as if I was running, I would have headaches, I would have throbbing pains all over, and my blood pressure would reach highs of epic proportions. After I left my job because I could barely function in such a high stress job, I decided that I needed to quit the medication. Little did I know that the worst of it was just about to start, as I had become addicted to the pills that were supposed to be helping me.

The class of medications I was prescribed are called benzodiazepines. The most common drug of this classification has the name Xanax. Now these medicines, if you do any research, are only to be used for a short duration. They are more addictive than heroin, and they have the worst withdrawal of any drug. I was about to try and come off of them on my own. When I decided to get off of them, I decided to just go down slowly. Little did I know that you have to taper down so slowly that it could take a full year to get off of them. The more research I did, the more scared I got. Benzodiazepines are one of two withdrawals that can actually kill you, alcohol being the other one. On several occasions, I was convinced I was going to die or that the unbearable pain I was in would never go away. There I was, an engineer, a commercial helicopter pilot, and even a successful triathlete, curled up in a ball in my shower crying my eyes out. I would shake uncontrollably for weeks, I never slept, I would sweat profusely every waking moment, and went on to lose significant weight because I couldn't keep anything in.

During this whole time, I had no support. My family was convinced I was either making this up or that I was just a drug

183

addict. I made it through the first month of pure hell and decided to go back to PachaMama to do the cleanse program to finally rid my body of the medication. Benzos are fat-soluble and stay in your system for a long time. It took over six weeks and a juice fast to finally come back negative on a store-bought drug test. This is where I connected with Rob, back in Costa Rica during one of the worst times of my life. I felt conformable opening up about what had happened and everyone was beyond supportive. I was not used to this at all.

After months of struggle, I started to feel better, but the sleep issues were still there and some of the symptoms I thought were part of the withdrawal were not getting better. I ended up seeing a functional medicine doctor, and instead of treating my symptoms, she looked for the underlying cause. Turns out, this entire time I had Lyme disease, and I am currently in treatment.

For a long time, I was upset with doctors, friends who disappeared, family members who kicked me while I was down, and even myself, but I am now trying to treat this whole experience as a blessing. I have the opportunity to completely change my life for the better, and possibly give back where I can. This whole experience has taught me to listen to my heart and stop worrying that I am breaking the mold I thought I had to conform to. Most of my family members are extremely unhappy people, and I refuse to live my life like that. I have wasted a lot of time being miserable, so I plan on packing the years I have left with things I love to do.

14

Southern California
Rob's Awakening Moment

It was hard to leave the town of Nosara, Costa Rica, as it held such a special place in my heart. However, there were only a few days left before my class on herbal medicine began, and I had to make the journey to the other side of the island. It took three buses and thirteen hours to get to the Caribbean side of the island to a city called Manzanillo. This was the town where the boat would pick us up to take us to Punta Mona for the class. The beaches on the Caribbean side of the island were very different from those on the Pacific side. The waves appeared much stronger.

The morning of our first day of class, I participated in an herbal walk led by the woman in charge of the place I was staying. To my surprise, there were two other classmates doing the walk as well. It was a great introduction to what I was about to embark on. It amazed me to walk through the small town and learn of all the herbal plants growing alongside the road, most of which you could eat. I was excited for the upcoming class.

Later that day, the boat picked us up and we all headed to Punta Mona. Punta Mona is a very unique place that offers permaculture classes and herbal studies. The entire property has herbs and medicinal plants everywhere you walk. It is an herbalist's dream. Over the next week, I was immersed in a training class, learning all I could absorb in regards to herbal medicine as it applied to first aid. We learned hundreds of herbs within such a short time. I felt as if my head were going to burst with all the information. I was enjoying every minute, but it was a lot of information to take in within a short time. We only had a week to learn the information, as the next week we would be setting up and running the herbal first aid clinic at the festival.

I felt so blessed to be able to be sitting in Costa Rica, learning this information I had yearned to know. It was another moment of following my dreams. This is what individuals in the past used; since they did not have pharmaceuticals, they used plant medicine. I was excited and yet nervous to head to the festival. I was excited to put what I had learned to practical use, but at the same time I was also nervous about not knowing everything. Fortunately, we had mentors and teachers there to supervise us and answer our questions.

We arrived at the festival grounds three days before the festival began so we could set up the clinic and treat the staff that were already there working. It was amazing to witness and be a part of the setup for a first aid clinic that was in the middle of a jungle, but also next to a beach. I had worked in many clinics and hospital settings in my career as an occupational therapist, but this was so unique and fun. Our tent was set up right next to the medic tent, so we could work in collaboration with them. This was something I thoroughly admired – the two tents working together, combining their medical and alternative health approaches.

Over the next six days, I worked a four-hour shift each day. The clinic was super busy. From the moment I walked in to the moment I left, there was a continuous flow of people seeking care. I loved how individuals were seeking alternative ways to heal their bodies. It was also fascinating to witness some of the same people coming back each day to get another dose or do a checkup, or to see them walking around the festival; they would often stop and say how much better they were feeling. We treated all kinds of ailments, including anxiety, pain, headaches, infections, fevers, sores, cuts, open wounds, sore throats, burns, etc. I saw huge improvements in people's health in such a short time period, using only medicinal herbs. It made my heart happy to witness such beauty occurring. In addition, this herbal first aid clinic that we were running was free of charge. Yes, free for all individuals to access. Wow, I had never witnessed such a thing. To have an herbal clinic at a festival was such a phenomenal idea, and to have it be free was such an added bonus. Not only were we serving all that came through, but we were educating them as well.

I am forever grateful that I was guided to this experience. To begin to learn herbal medicine and get some practical experience putting it to use was the best combination for me at that time. This, again, was sparking something deep within me. This was a spark that I had not felt in quite some time. I knew deep down there was still a missing piece as to how I was going to use this new knowledge; however, I was still thankful for the new awakening within me.

By the time I left the festival, I was exhausted. I had been camping for almost two weeks. I wanted a bed, a shower, and hot water. I booked a room for three days in the town closest to the festival, recouping and catching up on messages. At this point, I had about two weeks left on my three-month visa. I had a deep desire to go back to Nosara, the town I had fallen in love with before. Therefore, I took a week to travel along the coast to make it back up there. When I arrived there, it felt comforting again. However, the next day, I got very sick. I spent the next four days in bed, resting and recovering. I saw a doctor because I was running a high fever for a few days, and he said that I might have picked up a virus at the festival. I let it run its course, took the herbs I had, and gave my body the rest it needed.

That was not how I had imagined spending my last week in Costa Rica. However, I was feeling much better my last few days there, so I stayed at Bodhi Tree Yoga Resort. That place was out-of-this-world amazing. It was a perfect end to my trip. While there, I was able to reconnect with and attend a sound immersion meditation class. I had done this before, when I was in Nosara a month ago. Lying there listening to the quartz crystal bowls brought tears to my eyes. It brought back yet another deep passion within me. Before I left on my adventures almost two years prior, I had a wellness center wherein we offered this exact same thing – weekly shamanic sound immersions. The days that we offered this class were my favorite days of the week. I had seen over the years how sound is universal. Most people enjoy sound and music. However, some have difficulty with meditation. Therefore, these classes allowed a person to simply lie down and listen to the sound harmonics of these instruments, which then places his/her body in a relaxed state. The body enters a deep state of relaxation, similar to that of meditation. When in this state, deep healing can occur. People would report that their stress, back pain, migraines, and other ailments would disappear following an immersion. I was seeing that music and sound were gateways for people – gateways to access a place of deeper knowing and healing within themselves.

Therefore, listening to the sounds of the bowls again reignited the passion I had for playing these sacred instruments. That was it. That was the missing link from before. This was the second time in a two-week period that I had a spark within me. The first was from using medicinal herbs, and the now this one came from using sound frequencies. I thought to myself, *"How can I combine these two passions together?"* I immediately had the vision of recording plants to listen to their frequency. We are all made of energy, so why not record the voice of plants? This would allow people to listen to the vibrational frequency of a plant that has medicinal properties.

Wow, what a gift to have this new vision and spark just as I was completing my time in Costa Rica and other travels around the globe. As much as I loved Nosara, I was being guided back to California. I had contemplated renewing my visa and staying, as I was offered some opportunities. However, I did some meditations for clarity around the next step, and knew it was time to move forward. I also knew that if I needed to, I could always come back. Up until this point, I had always been guided in the right direction for my highest and greatest good – no need to stop trusting it now.

I had been in contact with my friend Dustin and told him that I was coming back to California to reevaluate the energy there.

He had told me that he had just finished a job and was going to be traveling down the coast of California as well. Therefore, I joined him in Santa Cruz, and together we headed down the California coast. It was wonderful to see him again.

When we got to Venice Beach, I reunited with my friend Stephen as well. Things were coming full circle. I found out that Stephen had been recording plants as well, using them in his sound lounge he had created. I loved it. Things were continually aligning.

Next, I reached out to my friend Rob Nicholas. He used to live close by, and I wanted to see if he was still in the area. I had met Rob at a CranioSacral Therapy course back in Michigan, years prior. He had been a student attending the course, and I was a teaching assistant for the class. When I met him, I couldn't help but notice that he had such a spark about him. His personality shined so brightly, and he was calm and joyful. During the four-day class, we became good friends.

Following the class, we stayed in contact. We would occasionally meet up for hikes or trade sessions with each other. However, about five years ago, Rob made the decision to move to California. I wished him well and knew that we would still stay in contact. Therefore, two years ago when I was in California checking out the area, I had reached out to him. We had met and again traded CranioSacral Therapy sessions. It was such a highlight to reconnect with such a beautiful soul. I always felt at ease when I was around Rob. We could spend hours just talking about life and the beauty of it all. He shared a very similar outlook and a positive perspective that I appreciated.

As this book has shown, I never ended up moving to California two years ago. Instead, I ended up on this amazing journey around the globe. However, I was now being guided back to where I had started – full circle. Rob was surprised to hear that I was back in California, as last he knew I was overseas somewhere. Schedules aligned and we met up, connecting right where we left off last time. It was that simple with him.

We both laughed in amazement at the unfolding of life. Here I was, sitting with Rob, enjoying a beautiful conversation just like when I had started my journey two years ago. He laughed, as he had just gotten inspired to start doing CranioSacral Therapy sessions again. Therefore, we traded sessions once again.

I am forever grateful for meeting Rob years ago through the work of CranioSacral Therapy. Life was guiding me back to California for a reason, and one of those reasons was to reconnect with this amazing soul. Rob's gifts shine so naturally with all his interactions. He creates such a sense of ease when in his presence. I honor his positive outlook and embodiment of joy.

Things were coming together easily and effortlessly. Rob's awakening moment could have been shared at the beginning of this book, as I had met him before going to Egypt, but I could not think of a better way to conclude this book than to share his story at the end. Full circle.

I was coming full circle in life once again. *"Where is life going to take me now?"*, I had thought to myself. I just embarked on a journey of a lifetime. I had come to realize that when I believe and live from a place of infinite trust, life beautifully aligns. I feel blessed to have expanded my community to a global capacity. As I allowed myself to be me, I met other individual men that were expanding into their truth. We together were breaking the boundaries of what society previously had defined as "masculinity." This awakening male consciousness that I was witnessing and experiencing was one that found strength in men expressing their emotions in a healthy manner. It allows for men to be present and step into their full potential. I will be forever grateful for the experiences expressed throughout this book and each individual man who came forth to share in the message. Together we can create and be the change.

Here is Rob's awakening moment:

Hello. Am I awake? Usually I rise quite gently in the morning. A slow but resolute process that's more reminiscent of wind and water incrementally breaking earth and making mountains eternally, than the all-at-once demolition of a sudden avalanche of heart-beating, cold-sweating consciousness. Gradual. A motif that's as consistent for me as the sun and moon are to the earth. Like gears in the clock of the universe that simply rely on an unquestioned intuition that flows like layers of wind, traipsing and weaving on and around a copse of numberless, nacreous birch. But I suppose there is an eclipse from time to time. The sun warms, the moon pulls, I erode and awaken gradually; an experience that ranges from contented stillness to overwhelming exhaustiveness. Rollercoastering up and down. It's a funny feeling... it's an enigmatic experience.

My name is Rob. My head has freed itself from my pillow, and I'm exploring the warm side of my southern California morning. A morning prefaced by a deep slumber belied by bullying dreams. As the alcohol from the night before aches its way through my body, I feel as though I've made it from my bedroom to the bathroom steered by sound, and into the kitchen by feel, without having yet opened my eyes. And when I do, the counter in the kitchen displays the dregs of an inebriated experience. Wine bottles (acquired from work), dirty glasses (not acquired from work), and stale streaks of many yet-to-be-identified dried-up liquids. The humming of vibration breaks the fuzzy yet idle quiescence of my hungover morning and I note the name and message from a long-unseen friend displayed on my phone. Bali? I thought he was moving here, to California. Thailand?!?!? I don't... what the... huh?

Impaired faculties don't allow me to stay very long on the line of thinking this message prompted, so I must move on to the necessary accoutrement of the disabled morning: caffeine, water, and recumbent darkness. While laying back, I get a feeling reminiscent of a time in my life when I felt, like a hillside being blindsided by an indifferent

breeze, my own rubble beginning to break and recede; when my mind
betrayed my body and a six-month-long uninterrupted panic attack
ensued. Saved by booze (not really, but it was surely a tool I utilized),
Xanax (I'm so fuckin' hesitant to say that it helped, but it did.
Pharmaceuticals have their place; motherfuckers are shady though –
keep an eye out), and a lot of bodywork (CranioSacral, shaman
healing, reiki, etc). Though here in this moment, in this slow,
shadowy morning, it's simply impulsiveness and bad decision-making
coming back to reap their full side of the bargain from the night before
that's making me feel so uneasy. Back then (during the attack, that
is), it seemed to come from nowhere and everywhere at the same time,
without my knowledge and most certainly without my permission. I
find the subtlety and duration of the unfolding of my later awakening
(though I hesitate to use this term) to be quite fitting. Though as we'll
see, the electric darkness (a phrase I'm still figuring out if I like – I'm
pretty sure I don't) that I've experienced (three times) in the past,
seems anything but subtle or controllable. A sort of in-your-face,
can't-do-anything-about-it, go-fuck-yourself helplessness, in fact.

There was a foreshadowing of events to come. A dipping-the-toe-
in-the-water sort of experience; though with the level of electricity
seemingly involved in this process, it is perhaps best to keep all water
metaphors to the side for now. Electric darkness. A blackout?
Glucose? Without the benefit of hindsight or medical tests, all
arguments were pure conjecture, but let us get to the event itself.
2004 or 2005. San Francisco. Fog. A day spent with vodka (I do want
to go on record here as stating that it was indeed a very modest
amount of alcohol), cannabis (same here in regards to dosage), and
multiple crab traps. As the afternoon was taking its last breaths,
waving goodbye to everyone and gradually receding into the night
and releasing itself to the silvery pale flames of the moon, like a ship
falling towards the horizon, I walked into the small dense San
Franciscan apartment of a friend, bringing with me the piscine
redolence of an afternoon spent wrestling metal cages from the bottom
of the ocean near an odd-numbered pier. Approaching the kitchen
counter with our day's catch not far away, it happened. Blackness. In
an instant, with no forewarning, all went dark. The rapidity with
which consciousness left and came back cannot be overstated. The

lights turned on before I even hit the floor. From curled on the floor to pulling myself back up to my feet, it's difficult to describe exactly what went wrong. To this day I'm not entirely sure. All engines shut down. Power was lost, though only for an instant. No shaking. Writing now with hindsight, it seems to me that my brain, every so often, without my knowledge or consent, reboots... ctrl, alt, del... with varying levels of severity.

Besides knocking my head on the corner edge of the counter, the bodily damage was nil, and to be honest, my thoughts in general were rather flippant about the whole thing. In hindsight, I can understand one's concern over dismissing an experience that jarring. All I can say is that I was young. Perhaps the best excuse for anything. As previously mentioned, this was merely the foreshadowing to the real electric light show that would commence three times from this point onward. It would be another year before the first of three seizures, which sent my head into a whirlwind.

The first one? Whooooooweeeeeee!!! Yeah... that'll pull your awareness from depression to self-preservation in an instant. Light. Spark. Perhaps a different spark than the one that may be being referenced in the context of this book. Perhaps not. But look at that, we've already drifted away, in almost the same instant, to put the cart in front of the horse. It all started as it probably fucking should have... at a roller coaster park. Cedar Point. Ohio. Cousins. Let's, for the purposes of this story, call them Nel and Cal. My cousins from Orlando, Florida. There are a few consistent variables from the preliminary test drive. Cannabis. A bit of booze. All of which were, once again I stress, very moderate in dosage. I was driving, for Christ's sake. But hold on a second... let's slow this cart down even more. Take it back to some of my favorite stuff in the world. Let's take it back to some Greek stuff. Not too much, because it's much too much to talk about here. But it certainly needs to be addressed, as it relates to the given subject matter – and even if it doesn't, I'm going to do it anyway because it's fun. And it makes me smile.

Nel and Cal Savadedes. From my dad's side. Something about our fathers sharing a grandmother. The old days in Detroit that the elder

193

Greeks would talk about. Stories perhaps a bit contrived, but more so from waxing nostalgic about Greek immigrant lore than any attempt at deception. Emotions trumping factual accuracy. Nel and Cal, sons of my dear uncle James. The only name besides my own that has not been changed. Because my uncle James is a wonderful human being, and he knows he wants the recognition anyway... and he deserves it. I love you, Uncle Jimmy. Yes, I grew up Greek. Both parents. Same village. A culture and religion so intertwined that I associate my religious upbringing as much with living loved ones as I do dead prophets. Social and spiritual. Both emotionally impactful. Both significant. Balancing the physical and metaphysical.

Back to the matter at hand. Nel and Cal came from Orlando, Florida (soon to relocate to Portland, Oregon – yes, both of them), to visit my family in Michigan. Spring in the middle aughts. Rollercoasters and storm clouds. The first alarm. They traveled from Orlando to Detroit. We traveled from my little town in Michigan to Sandusky, Ohio to explore the towering metal forces of noise and the rumble-tumble pathway of various wheels on tracks under shackled bodies... going fast. There were two portions to this day separated not pre-and post-seizure; but pre- and post-rainstorm. A storm that shifted the weight of the air from effervescent clarity to the moist denseness that seems to always be haunting the Midwest in the early summer months. Did the storm do it? Getting jostled on a few rollercoasters for an hour or so? The beer I drank? Alas, this is not the place for conjecture or open discussion. As more and more time went on, the question "Why?" seemed less and less significant, anyway. Why.

As generally happens at places like this, we spent a great deal more time waiting in lines than we did rapidly flying around metal and wood structures with closed eyes above giant smiles with flowing hair behind. And it was standing in line, after the tempest had sung, that I got my first taste of how nasty and unforgiving this thing was and would continue to be. Besides a cold sweat and an initial feeling of lightheadedness, there was no warning. And even the perspiration and head stuff didn't even give me enough time to consider them before I went out. Experience without consideration.

194

Standing alone, I slammed a railing on my direct descent to the still moist concrete my hand would slam into. I'm told the shaking was quite violent. They say the most dangerous part of a seizure is injuring yourself on the way out, like hitting your head, or biting your tongue, or something like that. I don't know. The brain suddenly going black and shutting down for a period of time (a time which would increase with each episode) and the lack of oxygen seem to be a hazardous part of the deal as well, and if not more injurious, certainly more of a mindfuck. A certain tension stemming from the fact that your consciousness seems to walk a very fine line. A slippery slope. Stillness and darkness ever-present somewhere in the recesses of my mind. Signal lost. Potentially paranoia inducing. Lying on the ground, my eyes lifted open but my mind stayed dark. Sight without context. Silence and ignorance in their purest forms.

Many downcast heads hanging in concern, with doleful eyes on long faces looking down at me; and I knew nothing. My hand was bleeding, and it hurt. I knew that, but as for anything else? My name? Where I was? No idea. "The year! Ask him what year it is," someone howled. It took a good half an hour for the majority of my memory to come back. In these circumstances, it is usually the ambulance ride from the point of attack to the hospital that most of my memory returns. The one memory that has never come back? The place I go when all goes black. I don't have any recollection of that unconscious time, and I don't know if there's an experience at all. Kind of like waking from a long slumber and not having dreamt. I'm not sure if nothing happened, or if I just forgot it all the second before reawakening... I'm not sure which I would prefer. After hours at the hospital and many apologies to Cal and Nel (both of whom asked me to stop apologizing), I went home with no real information about what had happened. Nel drove. Cal sat shotgun. I laid down in the backseat of my dad's Buick. It would be years before we would all be back together. It would be up in Portland, Oregon, after I had commenced my second attempt at living on the California coast. It would also be after the last stop-drop-and-shake episode. An event that nearly stymied my life in a life-threatening and insidious way. Not life-threatening in the sense that I would literally die (although who knows – I was convinced of it for a while), but it certainly would *have threatened a life worth living. Meaning. Choice. Once again, I'm not sure which is worse. But we'll get to that in a bit. We have a few more things to get through first.*

The earth had barely made its cosmic sojourn through its annual schedule of equinoxes and solstices before another episode came back around. Foreign land this time. Heathrow Airport. Followed up by a two-month romp around the European continent. Shit… I was already there and I didn't see any reason to go back home. Again, I know it can seem like a rather flippant reaction to what should be considered a life-altering experience. But stubborn youth, a bit of frustration, and, as will be discussed later, my given environment drove me forward.

It began with the energized decision of four young men to travel the European continent for two months because, well, I think it's pretty obvious. I traveled in big metal containers over vast spaces of various blues, solo, with the intention of meeting my trio of companions in Strasbourg, France. As you can imagine, I was late for our rendezvous. Alone and excited, my adventure came to an absolute and abrupt cessation. Blackness blended with electrical humming and a metaphysical traveling of some sort. Sometimes I wonder what would have happened had I not missed my flight. Would it have happened on the plane? Would it not have happened at all? The longer I live, the less I consider these sorts of questions. Instead, now I usually just smile and chuckle to myself and let go even further into the abyss. Smiling and laughter always a good remedy for such slippery self-talk.

It was the fiendishly circuitous security-check line that made me miss my flight from Heathrow to Frankfurt (it was from Frankfurt to Strasbourg that I was to meet my friends, by way of a train). It was from one airport gate to another that I would get my next gut check. After missing my connecting flight, I had another few hours to busy myself before connecting with my travel companions. As it turned out, I would have plenty to keep me busy.

No cannabis involved this time, though I did have a single glass of wine (used more for somnolence than anything else) on the eight-hour

196

flight over big blue water. Tobacco, however, would make its first entry into our story and it brought with it a consequence not normally attached to it. And this is no attempt at defending tobacco, but this shit was coming, cigarette or not. As with so many things, it was just timing. I had emerged from the fuliginous enclosure of one of the many smoking sections in Heathrow, billows of gray dancing beyond and behind me as I whisked through fresh air, a wake of fetid shadowy haze lingering aft, as I go from voluntary bad habit to involuntary shaking. I remember striding with bag over shoulder and blobs of clothing flashing by under bright oppressive airport lighting, where shadows don't exist. Cold sweat. Funny feeling. Out... Instantly (as it seemed to me, but from what I was told later, I was out and shaking horribly for over a minute) I reawakened to confusion, wet khakis, and people who talk funny... Same concerned slumping heads. Same shocked faces. I had the same answer for all the same old questions... "I don't know."

With each episode, I will admit I slowly began to realize the severity of what I was potentially dealing with; a susceptibility that could strike at any moment, without notice, and, given not necessarily unlikely circumstances, cause death. Despite the rocking of my consciousness, after many hours at some hospital in London, I hailed a cab from the hospital to the airport and caught my flight to Frankfurt. Train to Strasbourg. To this day, one of my favorite moments in my life was seeing my three friends' faces at the train station in Strasbourg. I think I finally could exhale. Relax. And hug people I loved. It was youthful exuberance and, to be honest, lack of any better options that moved me forward through Europe, not any sort of meaningful precedent made through choice. Not much clout as it were. But a profane frustration was certainly being rooted in my life, sprouting from the vulnerability that stems from the devastating and despoiling CNS shock and shutdown. Electric tension that can crumble the strongest of wills.

There was a long stretch of time between two and three. Enough time to haphazardly fall into an education that would prove to make more beneficial advancements personally than professionally. And perhaps save me from so many shades of darkness that meandered around my head and heart. Or at least give me a few more tools in the toolbox of assuaging my own discontentment. Massage school. Little did I know, this education would be the addition to the foundation that I needed in stabilizing an otherwise wobbling structure. (It was perhaps the impetus for the aforementioned panic attack, but that is still conjecture at this point. Also, it should be noted that there were many positives in coming out of such an experience.) A meandering mind back and forth, like dazzling green foliage dancing in the wind, from blackness to paranoid stillness. It was at massage school that I was introduced to an energetic world that would serve to facilitate clarity and confirmation. A world from which I had felt very separate. Gradually, it broke down obsolete structures and caused a shift in perspective that freed my mind in a myriad of ways. Erosion. Regrowth. It was here that I was introduced to CranioSacral work by the founder of our school, Irene Gauthier, whose ninetieth birthday we celebrated while I was studying there, which should be noted for having (at the time) set the record for longest human massage chain. It is also through this work that I came to meet the wonderful writer of this here book you're reading now; the same man who sent me the aforementioned text message from halfway across the world to my hungover apartment. Not to mention that this (CranioSacral work, that is) is the work that helped me recover from a six-month-long period of unfettered anxiety that wrapped itself around me like ivy on a wall. Suffocating.

In the long, slow process of my awakening (see earlier parenthetical in regards to the use of this term) the seizing broke me down. This education helped with the regrowth. The scab to the wound. Stronger. Tools that catalyze good decision making and ease worry (inasmuch as worries can be eased.)

Those still reading out there that are fans of arithmetic will not be surprised to hear that we have one last BURN-OUT-LIGHTS-OUT-SHAKE-QUAKE-TREMBLE spark to explore. It was a big one. The biggest. Beet-purple and oxygen-deprived, I still proceeded to move westward afterwards. Toward the place I'd meet back up with my friend writing this book. Coming full circle, as so many of these things tend to do. The palpable repercussion of riding waves instead of trudging and plodding against them. But back to our crescendo of shaking electricity. A road trip story. From Michigan to California. I decided to give the west coast another shot, with a more southern part of the state in mind. Coffee. A portly 2008 Mercury Sable overstuffed with the material items I felt necessary enough to take with me (my head stuffed with its own baggage) from a home rooted in a wonderful life of memories, moving forth to a new, unknown, yet-to-be-found home, neighboring the largest body of water in the world. Salty.

The saltwater began well before I reached the California shoreline. Pulling out of a driveway that I knew every crack and crevice of, I departed with a familiar face (saltwater slowly and hesitantly sloughing down my own face), towards an unknown that brought with it its own set of bewilderments. With a face I'd known since early childhood, I departed for unknown waters. Driving from the garage to the end of the driveway seemed to take hours. The longest fifty yards I've ever experienced. Before the trip officially began, we took a quick detour to the natural landscape of my own backyard. We didn't get to the fen (a venerated place amongst my close group of peers that grew up in the area), though we were close enough to feel its farewell and she blessed us both as I took a few pre-departure puffs of potent weed. And we were off, eyes shifting from wet and salty to dry and fiery red, dregs of dried salt settling into creases of squinting eyes under the late morning light of an April sun.

As it pertains to the scenery or conversation, there's nothing much of note between Michigan and Colorado (which is where my companion was to depart for his own festivities and leave me solo for the last thousand miles or so, a part of the plan I was looking forward to... the solo entrance into my new environment). From a strong foundation of people, places, and things, I had one last person to send me off to create whatever it may be that I would create for myself. It was through the gauntlet of Nebraskan corn fields that a storm began to gain steam. Dark clouds forming and moving faster than seems probable, as they tend to do in this part of the country. The Heartland. At this point I really felt like my mind started playing tricks with me as it pertains to my own environment. Creating a phantom-like experience, where it was difficult to pin down what was real and what

199

was manufactured by some giggling man behind the curtain of my brain. Was the car burning something it shouldn't be? Was that just the fetid remnants of cattle and fertilizer that is ubiquitous in this place? What was that smell? We stopped and looked at the car which seemed to show no signs of needing repair and proceeded westward as the storm continued to pick up speed and drop down hail. It was building and building until eventually we stopped the car at a McDonald's that was somewhere along, or close to the border of Colorado and Nebraska, along Interstate 80. Seizing in a fucking McDonald's. For those of you keeping track that's, a rollercoaster park, an international airport in a foreign land, and now a fucking McDonald's.

As we entered, we were welcomed by bright and offensive lights, that familiar fragrant fryer aroma, and other patrons (not interested in being patrons, but instead simply looking for shelter from the storm). I do, however, believe we (my friend and I) bought a couple ninety-nine cent ice cream cones and struck up conversation with a few of the others. It was at this point I saw a man with jacket, badge, and gun, and figured I would try to procure any information about the severity of the storm and anything else that may be helpful. Guys with the officiality that these raiments usually symbolize seem to have a lot of information others don't, or, perhaps, access to information that others don't. Or, at least, make regular Joes like me feel warm and fuzzy with reassuring words and gestures. He seemed optimistic, and I went back out to the car, through the heavy rain and ululating wind to grab a cigarette, which I instantly sparked up while hiding under the slight awning proffered by the extended roof of the clown's castle. This is pretty much the last thing I remember before it all went black. Apparently, I did walk back inside. Then. My mind went black, my skin went purple. I'm told the shaking was quite violent. Then. Silence. Stillness. Emptiness. Then from this nothingness to being birthed into the burger-slinging bright lights of the embodiment of American consumption. Eyes open. Brain closed for business. Same heads slumping. Same long faces. Different heart.

There was something different this time. I could feel it. Shaken and stirred. It was a full day before I felt even close to being back to normal. I awoke with the aches and pains of a heavyweight fighter. Life had doled out some punches, and I had taken my lumps. Foggy with a chance of remarkable pain and terror. There are two things that I remember most post-seizure. One, the face of my friend, Mick. And two, a conversation I had with my brother on the phone, connecting from middle-of-nowhere-middle-America to Beijing, China, where he was working.

I've never seen anybody seize. I'm told it's one of the scariest things in the world to witness, especially if it's someone you love (to this day I'm grateful neither of my parents have had to see it happen to me). Mick was visibly shaken. His voice. His eyes. My stop-drop-and-shake messed him up good. And it was partially this third person perspective from someone so close that instilled a much less flippant response, on my part, to this quite serious thing. Granted, the magnitude of this particular event along with the still-resonating waves from the shaking had made its own significant impact. His trembling description of events hit me on an emotional level where I had no choice but to seriously consider what was wrong with me and what I should do.

I love my brother. I love all of my siblings. I'm the youngest of four. The best spot to be, and perhaps the biggest reason why I've grown into the person who I've become… but back to my brother, the firstborn son; the matter-of-fact nature with which he speaks, especially as it pertains to important life-stuff, is quite a breath of fresh air. I don't recall the duration of our phone conversation, though I can't imagine it lasted very long. The question at hand, the question I was struggling with, was, "What the fuck do I do now?" I'm in the middle of nowhere, miles from anything of familiarity. Go back home? Was going to California still a viable option? Should I go home and get all the medical testing and information I needed to rid myself of this burden? I believe my brother put it in these terms: "What are you going to do – go home and live with Mom and Dad forever?" A bit of an overstatement, I would contend, but he wasn't wrong. He had also dipped a toe in the water himself, or perhaps an entire foot or two. To what extent was I going to allow this thing to dictate my life? Plus, all the medical testing I had received at this point gave me no answers, no specific diagnosis, and no relief outside of the suggestion of small, scary, insidious white pills that might not work and likely cause some brutal side effects. No thanks, doc. After three days of convalescence at altitude, in a cottage in the Colorado mountains, I drove through a rain-soaked windshield and a fog-filled head, shakily descending from the top of America to the sunny Pacific. Back to sea level.

My work now, five years later, is partly in the wine industry. My other work needs an entire other book to describe. Let's just say I'm a hiking guide and leave it at that for now. In my time working in the wine industry, there is something that people continually speak to me about. They describe to me their being in a foreign land, usually Italy or France, and how they had the most beautiful wine while sitting atop some Chateau, soaking up the relaxing, end of day, vermillion light glistening through varying apertures of waving limbs, storybook shadows fluttering across regal adornments. "Was the wine that spectacular?" they ask. Perhaps. But we must also include the context of the experience. The context of decisions being made. Adaptation to environment. The relationship between mindset and environment. Internal versus external. Or, perhaps more optimistically, internal dancing with external. And this leads into why this third knockout was of such significance. Not only because of its magnitude. But because of its placement in my life. Timing. It forced me to make a very important decision. To what extent could I afford to let this thing dictate my life?

A collision of experience and environment. Choice. A decision. A decision that impacted not just my current plans but was a jumping point from where I would set a rhythm of mindset that would beget either freedom or slavery depending on the choice made. Call it naiveté, call it ignorance, call it what you will, but it was at this moment that I first considered the proposition of how to truly make important decisions from good places. Pure and prudent intentions. Cause and remedy be damned, I was unfolding. Finding clarity and an unimpeded path to an inner (innate) knowledge. Empowerment. There was a strength acquired, or at least one that got its momentum initiated. A spark, perhaps. Puzzling. The thing I had no control over *made me realize the control I did have. The thing that happened in an instant forced a shift in the most gradual of processes. Avalanches and erosion. Balance. Libra. Scales. The sun and moon, juxtaposed, doing their due diligence and fulfilling their responsibilities to the universe. Intuition.*

Being now on this side of the experience, what do I think? What have I learned? The trouble with words is that they're merely symbols, and while tremendously useful and expressive, there's always something specific and significant that they can't quite capture, little bits and pieces getting lost in the expansive hazy gray. As it turns out, here on the warm side of the morning, the things that come to mind aren't the earth-shattering, soul-shaking, game-changing type stuff that I, and I'm assuming you, were hoping for. No... instead, the things that come to mind are the lame, hackneyed clichés everyone and their mother has heard over and over again; eye-rolling-type-shit that drives pupils towards ceilings and respect out the window. But there is something more. Something more that must hold us personally accountable. In the midst of it all, there is a constant and consistent opportunity for choice. An experience of making decisions. And it's a responsibility of great magnitude. To act and choose from an intuitive foundation of positive intentions... tune in. Choice. A responsibility that brings burdens and accountabilities, yes, but carries with it a tremendous sense of empowerment. Manifestation through prudent decision-making. A series of choices, a yoga-of-sorts that bends and brings together. Yoking the expanses of extremes with the knowledge that struggle precedes progress. Play. We are here; we might as well have some fun. Sincerity over seriousness. Muscles break to get stronger. Dance and stumble amongst the glorious gray that fills the gap from black to white. The gradual shifts, which inevitably shatter, direct collected attentions to the significance of direct experience. Every contour of her hand. Every salty Pacific breeze. Every speck of the rock. Uninhibited. Is it enough? When it's good... it's almost too much. Redolent. Resplendent. Resolute. It's a funny feeling... it's an enigmatic experience.

CPSIA information can be obtained
at www.ICGtesting.com
Printed in the USA
BVHW081412250219
541084BV00009B/518/P